CIVIL RIGHTS IN IMMIGRATION

CIVIL RIGHTS IN IMMIGRATION

By Milton R. Konvitz

Love ye therefore the stranger
(DEUTERONOMY 10:19)

We are commanded to honor and fear our parents. We are commanded to obey the prophets. A man may honor and fear and obey without loving. But in the case of strangers, we are commanded to love them with the whole force of our heart's affection.—Maimonides

GREENWOOD PRESS, PUBLISHERS
WESTPORT, CONNECTICUT

Library of Congress Cataloging in Publication Data

Konvitz, Milton Ridvas, 1908-
Civil rights in immigration.

Reprint of the ed. published by Cornell University Press, Ithaca, issued in series: Cornell studies in civil liberty.
Includes bibliographical references and index.
1. Emigration and immigration law--United States.
2. Civil rights--United States. I. Title.
II. Series: Cornell University. Cornell studies in civil liberty.
[KF4819.K65 1977] 342'.73'082 77-2605
ISBN 0-8371-9556-X

Originally published in 1953 by Cornell University Press, Ithaca

Reprinted in 1977 by Greenwood Press
A division of Congressional Information Service
88 Post Road West, Westport, Connecticut 06881

Library of Congress Catalog Card Number 77-2605

ISBN 0-8371-9556-X

Printed in the United States of America

10 9 8 7 6 5 4 3 2

For Horace M. Kallen and Sidney Hook

Preface

IN 1946 the Cornell University Press initiated the Cornell Studies in Civil Liberty with my book *The Alien and the Asiatic in American Law.* Since then many significant things have come to pass: the Supreme Court has decided cases that have an important bearing on immigration and nationality from the constitutional standpoint; Congress has enacted the Internal Security Act of 1950 (McCarran Act) and the Immigration and Nationality Act of 1952 (McCarran-Walter Act); two Presidents of the United States, Truman and Eisenhower, have condemned the policies of Congress and have called for legislation along new lines—laws which will be, said President Eisenhower, "faithful to our basic ideas of freedom and fairness to all."

I have not revised that book, but have written a completely new one. "To take up an idea again, consciously," Paul Valéry once said, "is to renew it, to modify, enrich, simplify or destroy that idea." In taking up the ideas of the earlier book, I have renewed, modified or destroyed them; some of the ideas I have left untouched, but for those the reader of this book is referred in appropriate footnote citations—they are not repeated here. For a study of the economic and cultural rights of aliens and of our treatment of Americans of Japanese ancestry in World War II, the reader can still find useful seven of the eleven chapters of the 1946 book.

Although this new book was written before President Eisenhower delivered his first State of the Union message, on February 2, 1953, my subject was defined by him. "There is one sphere in which civil rights are inevitably involved in Federal legislation," he said. "This is the sphere of immigration." This book is precisely about this sphere: civil rights in the McCarran-Walter Act, or discrimination on account of race, color, creed, opinion, or national origin in our legislation relating to the admission and exclusion of immigrants, deportation, and naturalization.

The book is intended as a contribution to the education of American citizens concerned with public affairs. It is not a monograph intended for the expert exclusively. I have assumed that there are many Americans, in and outside of our colleges and universities, who would like to have in a book of about sixty thousand words an objective, critical evaluation of American immigration policy, so that they might be enabled to decide for themselves what is right and what is wrong in that policy. I have assumed that they want to see the forest and have the intellectual and moral patience to see the trees, too, though they prefer to be kept out of the underbrush.

Though the reader will want to judge policies for himself, he will find that, while I have stated facts and arguments—I hope—fairly and objectively, I, too, have wanted to judge policies for myself. Just as an observer, we are told, can recognize Tintoretto among the figures in the "Paradise" or Veronese among the feastmakers in the "Cena di Levi," so the reader will recognize the author in many passages in this book. In discussions that touch closely questions of public policy, the need to seek answers to basic questions is one that exists for the writer no less than for the reader. "It is probable," Dr. Oliver C. Carmichael has said in his recent report as president of the Carnegie Foundation for the Advancement of Teaching, "that wholly neutral instruction weakens rather than strengthens the ability to make commitments, and yet an education that does not strengthen the power of conviction, that does not inculcate a sense of social responsibility, fails in its duty to society." The author of this book hopes that a reading of the book will strengthen the reader's power of conviction and his or her sense of social responsibility precisely because we have not avoided asking fundamental questions and because we have sought understanding as well as knowledge.

This book was almost completed when the report of the President's Commission on Immigration and Naturalization was made public. I have found most of my own views confirmed by that report, and have made changes in my footnotes so that the report will be found cited at appropriate points. The American people should feel a sense of gratitude for the work done by the Commission (especially of its chairman, Philip B. Perlman, former Solicitor General of the United States, and of its executive director, Harry N. Rosenfield, former member of the United States Displaced Persons Commission). With the Commission I agree that the national origins quota system should be abolished. I go a bit further than the Commission, however, in proposing reforms of our deportation system, so that it will be possible to expel only persons whose entry was fraudulent or illegal; in suggesting that the Administrative Procedure Act be made applicable to entry and exclusion, as well as deportation, cases; and in urging the elimination of all but the constitutional distinctions between native born and naturalized citizens. The differences between the Commission and me are only such as may be expected among persons who accept the same basic premises, yet reach slightly different conclusions, because some considerations receive in their thinking different degrees of emphasis.

In the context of a cold war that may turn into World War III, some readers probably will think that some of the ideals basic to the argument in this book are impossible ones. But Reinhold Niebuhr has reminded us that sometimes impossible ideals are also relevant. Ideals, I would add, are especially relevant when they seem impossible, for then they may compel us to raise our sights and to cease being completely preoccupied with facts and factuality. Loyalty to "impossible" ideals may be a key "to the kingdom which doth not yet appear."

This book is the result of studies conducted by me as a Faculty Fellow of the Fund for the Advancement of Education, established by the Ford Foundation. It represents, however, the independent work of the author, who alone is responsible for it.

While many college and university administrators give only lip service to the unity of teaching and research, in the administrative hands of Dean M. P. Catherwood this ideal has become an implemented policy, a plan of action. In expressing my gratitude to him I am but following the precept to thank the bridge that carries you over.

M. R. K.

New York State School of Industrial and Labor Relations
Cornell University
June 18, 1953

Contents

CONTENTS

CIVIL RIGHTS IN IMMIGRATION

CHAPTER I

Admission and Exclusion Policies

PLENARY POWER TO EXCLUDE

THE CHINESE exclusion acts of the 1880's presented the first opportunity to the Supreme Court to chart broadly the powers of Congress with regard to immigration and the exclusion from our shores of persons deemed, for one reason or another, or for no reason at all, undesirable. In the *Chinese Exclusion* case[1] the court, in a unanimous opinion, asserted constitutional propositions that are still judicially unchallenged.

The facts in this case were simple: A Chinese laborer had lived in this country for twelve years; in 1887 he left for China, and he had in his possession when he left a certificate from the government which purported to entitle him to re-enter the United States—a certificate which had been issued to him pursuant to 1882 and 1884 statutes. He returned in 1888 and presented his certificate, but he was refused admission because seven days before his arrival Congress had passed an act[2] by which outstanding certificates were annulled and his right to re-enter was abrogated. In a *habeas corpus* proceeding, the 1888 act was assailed as be-

[1] Chae Chan Ping v. U.S., 130 U.S. 581 (1889). For earlier cases, see Konvitz, *The Alien and the Asiatic in American Law* (1946), 8-9. *Cf.* generally Note, 66 *Harv. L. Rev.* 643 (1953).

[2] 25 Stat. 476 (1888).

ing in effect an order of expulsion in violation of treaties between the United States and China and in violation of rights vested in Chinese laborers living in the United States.

The Supreme Court, conceding that the statute was in contravention of express provisions of treaties, upheld its validity. Congress, said Mr. Justice Field for the court, may exclude aliens. If Congress "considers the presence of foreigners of a different race in this country . . . to be dangerous to its peace and security," though the countries are at peace, they may be excluded. The power to exclude foreigners, said the court, is an incident of sovereignty;[3] and this power is not subject to barter or trade; "whatever license" to return to the United States Chinese laborers might have obtained under treaties or acts of Congress previous to the act of 1888, was held "at the will of the government, revocable at any time, at its pleasure." The court in effect held that Congress had the power, unrestricted by constitutional limitations, to suspend or prohibit immigration of all foreigners or of the members of a particular race, nation, or group.

Congress may prohibit the entry of aliens because of their beliefs or opinions;[4] and persons excluded for this cause cannot plead the guarantees of the First Amendment: "those who are excluded cannot assert the rights in general obtaining in a land to which they do not belong as citizens or otherwise."[5] In brief, the power of Congress to exclude all or any class of aliens is plenary and not limited by the Bill of Rights or other constitutional provisions. Mr. Justice Murphy stated the proposition as follows: "The Bill of Rights is a futile authority for the alien seeking admission for the first time to these shores."[6]

This proposition has been affirmed and re-enforced by

[3] For discussion of this argument see Konvitz, *op cit.*, 12-20.

[4] Turner v. Williams, 194 U.S. 279 (1904).

[5] *Ibid.* For discussion of this case see Konvitz, *op. cit.*, 33-37.

[6] Concurring opinion in Bridges v. Wixon, 326 U.S. 135 (1945).

the decision of the court in the *Knauff* case, decided in 1950.[7] In the view of the court, as expressed by Mr. Justice Minton,

> an alien who seeks admission to this country may not do so under any claim of right. Admission of aliens to the United States is a privilege granted by the sovereign United States government. Such privilege is granted to an alien only upon such terms as the United States shall prescribe. . . . The exclusion of aliens is a fundamental act of sovereignty. The right to do so stems not alone from legislative power but is inherent in the executive power to control the foreign affairs of the nation.

In a case decided in 1952,[8] Mr. Justice Douglas, in a dissenting opinion, in which Mr. Justice Black concurred, argued that the power of Congress to exclude, admit or deport aliens flows from sovereignty itself and from the power delegated to Congress to establish a uniform rule of naturalization.[9] The power to deport aliens is, therefore, an *implied* one. But the right to life and liberty is an *express* one. "Why this *implied* power should be given priority over the *express* guarantee of the Fifth Amendment," said Douglas, "has never been satisfactorily answered."

What Douglas has said of the power to deport may also be said of the power to admit or exclude aliens; but he has not said it, nor has it been said by any other member of the court. The constitutional law with regard to the power of Congress to admit or exclude aliens is simply that the power is plenary; it is in no way restricted by the Bill of Rights.

RACIAL EXCLUSIONS UNDER IMMIGRATION LAWS

A pattern of racial exclusion in American immigration

[7] U.S. ex rel. Knauff v. Shaughnessy, 338 U.S. 537 (1950). Justices Frankfurter, Black, and Jackson dissented. Justices Douglas and Clark did not participate. The decision was 4 to 3.

[8] Harisiades v. Shaughnessy, 342 U.S. 580 (1952).

[9] U.S. Const., Art. I, sec. 8, cl. 4.

policy persisted for seventy years—from 1882 to 1952. The Immigration and Nationality Act of 1952 has brought almost to a close a chapter in the story of our immigration policy that one day will be read with disbelief. Americans of future generations will say: "No! it couldn't have happened here."

The first people to be excluded were the Chinese. In 1879 Congress passed a bill to exclude Chinese laborers. It was vetoed by President Hayes. In 1882 Congress passed another act, suspending Chinese immigration for twenty years. It was vetoed by President Arthur. Then Congress passed an act[10] to suspend Chinese immigration for ten years. This act was not vetoed and marks the beginning of our racial exclusion[11] policy. An act of 1892[12] extended the suspension for another ten years. In 1902[13] the policy became one of permanent exclusion, and the exclusion of Chinese immigrants continued until 1943.[14] Because of World War II, in which we were then engaged, and because China was our ally and was to be one of the Big Five of the United Nations,[15] Congress acceded to the request of President Roosevelt, who, in a message to Congress, said: "By repeal of the Chinese exclusion laws, we can correct a historic mistake and silence the distorted Japanese propaganda."[16]

Before the end of the nineteenth century there was agitation to exclude also Japanese aliens. Washington officials

[10] 22 Stat. 58 (1882).

[11] It should be noted that this act only *suspended* Chinese immigration. No absolute prohibition was enacted until 1902. See Konvitz, *op. cit.*, 4-22.

[12] 27 Stat. 25 (1892). [13] 32 Stat. 176 (1902).

[14] 57 Stat. 600 (1943).

[15] The Charter of the United Nations Organization was adopted June 6, 1945, but China's role as one of the great nations was indicated by previous events; e.g., the Moscow Declaration of October 30, 1943, was made by the governments of the United States, the United Kingdom, the Soviet Union, and China. This was only six weeks before Congress repealed the exclusion laws (December 17, 1943). F. W. Riggs, *Pressures on Congress* (1950), *passim.*

[16] Message of October 12, 1943.

were, however, hesitant about affronting Japan. Ways were sought to achieve exclusion without doing too much damage to relations between the two governments. President Theodore Roosevelt was successful in 1907 in effecting the so-called Gentlemen's Agreement with Japan, which provided for a virtual stoppage of Japanese immigration.[17]

The clamor, however, for a Japanese exclusion law did not abate. When the Supreme Court in 1922[18] held that the Japanese were ineligible for naturalization, the demand for a Japanese exclusion law began to take the form of a request for a law that persons ineligible for naturalization shall be excluded from admission as immigrants.[19] When the 1924 immigration act was under consideration, the groups that agitated for the conversion of the Gentlemen's Agreement into a congressional act succeeded in writing into the new law a provision that "No alien ineligible to citizenship shall be admitted to the United States."[20] Thus the immigration act of 1924 became also the Japanese exclusion act, though not *eo nomine.*

There was no need for this provision; it only added insult to injury. When the bill was pending in Congress, Charles Evans Hughes, as Secretary of State, pleaded for the exclusion of the provision. The Japanese, he said (echoing Theo-

[17] R. L. Garis, *Immigration Restriction* (1927), ch. x. Theodore Roosevelt in *An Autobiography* gives many of the details. He says: "Unfortunately, after I left office, a most mistaken and ill-advised policy was pursued toward Japan, combining irritation and inefficiency. . . . I cannot too strongly express my indignation with, and abhorrence of, reckless public writers and speakers who, with coarse and vulgar insolence, insult the Japanese people and thereby do the greatest wrong not only to Japan but to their own country. Such conduct represents that nadir of underbreeding and folly. The Japanese are one of the great nations of the world, entitled to stand, and standing, on a footing of full equality with any nation of Europe or America." National Ed. of the *Works* of Theodore Roosevelt (1926), XX, 371.

[18] Ozawa v. U.S., 260 U.S. 178 (1922). [19] See Konvitz, *op. cit.*, 22-25.

[20] 43 Stat. 153, sec. 13 (c) (1924); 8 U.S.C. 213 (c). Cf. 8 U.S.C. 224 (c) which defined the term "ineligible to citizenship."

dore Roosevelt), "are a sensitive people and unquestionably would regard such a legislative enactment as fixing a stigma upon them."[21] Hughes then added a sentence the full import of which was not apparent until December 7, 1941, when Japan attacked the United States at Pearl Harbor. He continued: "I regret that I feel compelled to say that I believe such legislative action would largely undo the work of the Washington Conference on Limitation of Armament." President Coolidge suggested delay;[22] his suggestion was turned down, and the bill was enacted with the exclusion provision in it. Coolidge signed the measure reluctantly. A few days later our ambassador in Tokyo resigned, saying: "The Japanese Government, I believe, would be willing to agree to almost any form of restrictive treaty, but the exclusion provision in the immigration bill has struck a blow to their natural pride."[23]

The Japanese government in a formal protest said:

It is, perhaps, needless to state that international discriminations in any form and on any subject, even if based on purely economic reasons, are opposed to the principles of justice and fairness upon which the friendly intercourse between nations must, in its final analysis, depend. . . . Still more unwelcome are discriminations based on race. . . . It is not denied that, fundamentally speaking, it lies within the inherent sovereign power of each state to limit and control immigration to its domains, but when in the exercise of such right, an evident injustice is done to a foreign nation in disregard of its proper self-respect, of international understandings or of ordinary rules of comity, the question necessarily assumes an aspect which justifies diplomatic discussion and adjustment.[24]

[21] Statement submitted to the chairman of the House Committee on Immigration; quoted in Y. Ichihashi, *Japanese in the United States* (1932), 300.

[22] Ichihashi, *op. cit.*, 309. [23] *Ibid.*, 314.

[24] *Ibid.*, 311-313.

The Japanese ambassador at Washington resigned. Fifteen leading newspapers in Tokyo published a joint denunciation of the act; there were anti-American demonstrations, including a boycott of American merchants and cinema films; and both branches of the Diet adopted a denunciatory resolution.[25]

In 1929 a Japanese leader said of the law: "It is not a closed incident. . . ." In the following year, Congressman Albert Johnson, author of the 1924 act, announced that he favored an amendment to repeal the exclusion provision and to give the Japanese a quota.[26] But nothing came of this. Relations between the governments deteriorated; the events at Pearl Harbor catapulted us into World War II.

The 1952 act, as we shall see, erased almost entirely the exclusion provision. No one is barred from naturalization today because of his race; no one is excluded from entry because he is ineligible for naturalization: the new law wipes out the category of racial ineligibility. But it is well not to forget these tragic blots on the American conscience; for, as Theodore Roosevelt said with regard to the exposure of slavery: "I think such exposure a good thing, for, as the evil no longer exists, people tend to forget how dreadful it was, and a few persons of warped morality tend to speak of it apologetically, or even in guarded praise."[27]

Immigration from the following countries, besides Japan, was excluded because natives from these countries were held to be ineligible for naturalization: Korea, Burma, Malaya, Polynesia, New Zealand, and Tahiti.[28] Chinese were excluded under special exclusion laws, as we have seen.

[25] *Ibid.*, 314-316. [26] *Ibid.*, 367, 369.

[27] Roosevelt, "The Negro in America," *Literary Essays* (National Ed.) (1926), XII, 214-216.

[28] Cf. *The Immigration and Naturalization Systems of the United States.* Senate Report 1515; Report of Senate Committee on the Judiciary; 81st Cong., 2d sess. (1950), 369.

In addition, by the "barred zone" provisions of a law enacted in 1917,[29] natives from the following places were excluded: India; parts of Russia, Arabia, and Afghanistan; Siam, and the East Indian Islands.[30]

The first rebuff to the racial exclusionary principle, as we have seen, came in 1943, when the Chinese exclusion laws were repealed. A second step was taken in 1946, when Congress enacted legislation [31] which provided for the admission of persons belonging to races indigenous to India and the Philippines. The third step was taken by Congress in the enactment of the Immigration and Nationality Act of 1952, which allegedly repealed all racial exclusionary provisions of our immigration laws, though characteristics of a racist policy remain.[32]

[29] 39 Stat. 874, sec. 3 (1917).

[30] Some peoples were barred under both the "barred zone" provision and the provision of the 1924 act which excluded immigrants who would be ineligible for naturalization. This was true, e.g., of the Chinese and the Burmese. See *op. cit. supra*, note 28, pp. 368-369. There is no uniformity among the various lists of excluded peoples. Cf. Konvitz, *op. cit.*, 26, and *Hearings on H.R. 5004* before Subcommittee on Immigration and Naturalization of House Committee on Judiciary, April 19 and 21, 1948, serial no. 18, p. 28.

[31] 60 Stat. 416 (1946). The Republic of Philippines was proclaimed on July 4, 1946. Congress passed the statute ending the prohibition on immigration from that country on July 2, 1946. Indian independence was imminent. On February 20, 1947, the British government announced its intention to partition India into two dominions.

[32] H.R. 199, 81st Cong., known as the Judd Bill, was passed by the House of Representatives, March 1, 1949. This measure, if it had been passed by the Senate, would have ended racial exclusion three years sooner.

It should be noted that two provisions of the 1952 act involve race discrimination. (1) Sec. 202 (b) concerns persons who are related by as much as one-half of their ancestry to peoples indigenous to an Asia-Pacific triangle defined by the act. Such persons "are charged to the countries of Asia, wherever they have been born, or however long their ancestors have made their homes outside the land of their origin." President Truman summarized, in his veto message, the provision in the law affecting persons of Oriental ancestry. "These provisions," he added, "are without justification." The rule would work this way: "a native of England whose parents were British by citizenship, but whose mother was Chinese by ancestry, must apply under the Chinese quota of 105, rather than under the British quota

It is interesting to note that among the organizations that favored the removal of racial bars to immigration were the American Legion and the Veterans of Foreign Wars of the State of California.[33] Despite our cold war with Communist China, no effort was made to make China an exception by repealing the 1943 act. The insult that had been offered the races and nations by the exclusion laws was a gratuitous one; for, had they been treated on a basis of equality with some European peoples, our quota laws would have been effective to keep immigration from the prohibited areas down to an annual total of about 1000 immigrants, including the Chinese and Japanese.[34]

Racial exclusion is no longer a conspicuous feature of our immigration policy. There is, however, flagrant national and religious discrimination. We now turn to a consideration of this topic.

---

of 65,000." *Economic Outlook* (C.I.O.), (November 1952), 76. Proponents of the bill have argued that without this provision, the United States might be "flooded" with Orientals now living in nonquota Latin-American countries. *New York Times,* June 28, 1952. There are no facts which show that this would be the case. Bars against the "flood" could be erected when the need for them is demonstrated. Although immigration from Central or South America is on a nonquota basis, Sec. 101 (A) (27), immigrants from these parts have not "flooded" the United States. From 1941 to 1949 only 19,496 persons were admitted from Central America, and only 18,547 from South America. During a period of 130 years, 1820-1949, the totals of immigrants from these two areas, respectively, were 68,650 and 139,849. *Op. cit. supra* note 28, Table 2, p. 816.

(2) While, previously, natives of colonial areas—e.g., Jamaicans—could enter within the quota of the mother country—e.g., Great Britain—now a limit of 100 has been placed on entries from any colony; cf. Sec. 202 (c). This provision affects primarily Negroes, whose immigration from the West Indies will be cut by about 90 per cent. "The Immigration Maze," *Christian Science Monitor,* December 29, 1952. The total immigration from the West Indies during the 130 years from 1920 to 1949 was 490,490. *Op. cit. supra* note 28, Table 2, p. 816. See statement of Walter White in *Hearings Before the President's Commission on Immigration and Naturalization,* 82d Cong., 2d sess., House Judiciary Committee (1952), 43-47.

[33] *Op. cit. supra* note 28, p. 371.

[34] R. D. McKenzie, *Encyc. Soc. Sciences* (1933), XI, 493.

DISCRIMINATION UNDER QUOTA LAWS

Until 1921 almost any person (except those subject to racial exclusion) in good physical and mental condition, and of good moral character, could enter the United States. In that year this policy was abandoned. The Quota Act of 1921[35] limited the number of immigrants to be admitted annually to approximately 350,000 (which was 3 per cent of the number of aliens of various nationalities resident in the United States according to the 1910 census). Each European country was assigned a fixed quota, as were also countries of the Near East, Africa, and Australasia. No overt racial, national, or religious distinctions were made in the law, but it was discriminating in practice; for, while it did not affect immigration from northern and western Europe, it effectively restricted immigration from southern and eastern Europe.[36]

Congress did not consider this law sufficiently stringent, so in 1924 it enacted a new statute,[37] the substance of which was incorporated into the McCarran-Walter Act of 1952. The statutory scheme was a complicated one; what it came down to was this. The total annual quota was to be about 154,000. This total was apportioned among the various countries to which the act applied according to the "national origins" formula, or their relative contribution to the American population as shown by the census of 1920.

The Senate Committee on the Judiciary, of which Senator Pat McCarran was chairman, and which sponsored the McCarran-Walter Bill, frankly admitted the discriminatory motivation of the 1924 act. The report of this committee, published in 1950, stated that the discussion and debates

[35] 42 Stat. 5 (1921).

[36] See M. R. Davie, *World Immigration* (1939), 375-376.

[37] 43 Stat. 153 (1924). This is the permanent quota law. It was to go into effect July 1, 1927, but the date was extended later to July 1, 1929.

centering around the adoption of the quota system and the national origins formula in 1924

leave little doubt that one of the motivating reasons behind the enactment of the law was the restriction of immigration from southern and eastern Europe in order to preserve a predominance of persons of northwestern European origin in the composition of our total population. The expressions of the proponents of the bill clearly indicate a belief in the necessity for the maintenance of a preponderance of strains of the early elements in our population if the fundamental institutions of the Nation were to be preserved and the superior position of the Nation maintained.[38]

The House Committee on Immigration and Naturalization, when it reported the decision of the committee to sponsor the 1924 measure, stated:

With the full recognition of the material progress which we owe to the races from southern and eastern Europe, we are conscious that the continued arrival of great numbers tends to upset our balance of population, to depress our standard of living, and to unduly charge our institutions for the care of the socially inadequate.

If immigration from southern and eastern Europe may enter the United States on a basis of substantial equality with that admitted from the older sources of supply, it is clear that if any appreciable number of immigrants are to be allowed to land upon our shores the balance of racial preponderance must in time pass to those elements of the population who reproduce more rapidly on a lower standard of living than those possessing other ideals. . . Late arrivals are in all fairness not entitled to special privilege over those who have arrived at an earlier date and thereby contributed more to the advancement of the Nation.[39]

[38] *Op. cit supra* note 28, p. 443. *Cf.* statement by Senator Reed, quoted in *Whom We Shall Welcome,* Report of President's Commission on Immigration and Naturalization (1953), 89.

[39] Report to accompany H. R. 7995, 68th Cong., 13-14, quoted in *op. cit. supra* note 28, pp. 60-61. *Cf.* statement of Oscar Handlin, *Hearings Before the President's Commission on Immigration and Naturalization,* 82d Cong., 2d sess. (1952), 327 and 1839.

Under the permanent quota law, Great Britain and Northern Ireland were given a quota of 65,721—the largest number under the law; next came Germany, with 25,957; then Ireland (later Eire) with 17,853. These three countries alone, then, enjoyed a combined quota of approximately 110,000, or about 72 per cent of the total.[40] The total for northern and western Europe was about 79 per cent of the combined quotas, the countries of southern and eastern Europe about 15 per cent.[41]

This apportionment scheme reflected agitation to base our immigration policy on racial and eugenic considerations. Publications appeared warning

> of the danger that the Anglo-Saxon stock would not survive in the United States if the present type of immigration continued. Heterogeneity of race in itself was coming to be considered harmful and the lack of assimilability of the south and east Europeans was often emphasized. This attitude was crystallized following the close of the [first world] war, when a wave of Nationalism swept over the country, in the development of racialism, a theory that culture is an expression of race and that some races are more highly endowed than others. A number of books were published devoted to the self-admiration of the white race and to the glorification of the Nordic branch. . . . Some such belief in the hereditary superiority of northern and western Europeans over southern and eastern Europeans, though based on ethnocentrism and emotionalism and not supported by science, underlay the support commonly given to restriction. Thus fear of racial deterioration was added to the other arguments in favor of restriction.[42]

The Report of the Senate Committee on the Judiciary in 1950 found that as a method for the numerical restriction of

[40] See Table 2 in *op. cit. supra* note 28, pp. 886-887.
[41] *Ibid.*, 445. The percentages may be 81.6 and 16; cf. *Whom We Shall Welcome,* 106.
[42] Davie, *op. cit.,* 372.

immigration, the system set in operation by the acts of 1921 and 1924 "has served its purpose well."[43] Under the national origins quota law, as it finally went into effect on July 1, 1929,[44] only 27 per cent of the available quotas have been used—836,085 quota immigrants have been admitted out of a total of 3,076,254 admissible under the law. When admissions are set off by departures, there was an average annual net increase to our population of only 22,000 for the years 1924-1946.[45] As a restrictive measure, then, the law "has served its purpose well." However,

> As a method preserving the relationship between the various elements in our white population, the national origins system has not been as effective.... Although the countries of northern and western Europe have continued to contribute the predominant number of immigrants under the quota system, the proportionate contribution of the various nationalities has departed from the ratios contemplated by the framers of the system [79 per cent from northern and western Europe, 15 per cent from southern and eastern Europe].[46]

From this standpoint the system has not been effective because "only about half the anticipated proportion of immigrants have come from northern and western Europe"; and from this area Germany, rather than Great Britain, has been the largest contributor. From 1924 to 1946 immigration from northern and western Europe constituted 43.1 per cent, instead of 79 per cent, of the total, and immigration from southern and eastern Europe constituted 18.9 per cent, instead of 15 per cent.[47] This disequilibrium in the proportionate distribution of admitted immigrants has not, how-

[43] *Op. cit. supra* note 28, p. 445.
[44] See note 37 *supra.*
[45] *Op. cit. supra* note 28, p. 445.
[46] *Ibid.*
[47] *Ibid.*, 445-446. Other interesting statistical figures are given on p. 446. See also *Hearings Before the President's Commission on Immigration and Naturalization,* table on p. 1893.

ever, seriously affected the national-racial-cultural pattern of the American people:

It would appear that the numerical restrictive feature of the formula, the economic depression, and the turmoil of war, have so limited immigration that there has been no significant effect on the homogeneity of our population because of the failure of the national origins formula to channel immigration in the desired proportions. . . . While immigration has not followed the pattern contemplated under the national origins formula, it has been of such small net volume during the effectiveness of the formula that it has not adversely affected the homogeneity of our population.[48]

In 1950, as in 1924, the Congress of the United States was preoccupied with "the need for preserving the balance of the various elements of our population."[49] If the national origins formula resulted in some countries having smaller quotas, this result followed "from the proportions in which aliens had previously entered the country. It may be true, as is alleged," said the Senate committee report, "that the quota laws were directed primarily at the restriction of immigration from southern and eastern European areas. That was, however, the area from which the greatest numbers were coming, thereby giving rise to the clamor for restriction." The formula that was evolved to meet the need for immigration restriction was both "logical" and "easily administered."[50]

The Immigration and Nationality Act, which went into effect December 24, 1952, perpetuates this formula and continues the computation of quotas among the various nations and areas of the world on the basis of the national ori-

[48] *Op. cit. supra* note 28, pp. 446, 447. For effect of 1924 act, see *Whom We Shall Welcome,* ch. 7.

[49] *Op. cit. supra* note 28, 448.

[50] *Ibid.*

gins of the American people as shown by the 1920 census.

This is the justification for continuing the national origins quota system offered by the Senate Committee on the Judiciary in its 1950 report:

> . . . . the adoption of the national origins formula was a rational and logical method of numerically restricting immigration in such a manner as to best preserve the sociological and cultural balance in the population of the United States. There is no doubt that it favored the peoples of the countries of northern and western Europe over those of southern and eastern Europe, but the subcommittee [of the Committee on the Judiciary] holds that the peoples who had made the greatest contribution to the development of this country were fully justified in determining that the country was no longer a field for further colonization, and henceforth, further immigration would not only be restricted but directed to admit immigrants considered to be more readily assimilable because of the similarity of their cultural background to those of the principal components of our population.[51]

That Congress was in no mood to tamper with the national origins formula is shown by the fact that the bill introduced by Senators Hubert H. Humphrey, Herbert H. Lehman, Paul H. Douglas, Estes Kefauver, Wayne Morse, and several others, also provided for national origins quotas, except that this bill used the census of 1950 instead of the census of 1920 as the base, and provided for the pooling of unissued and unused quota numbers.[52] These are admittedly significant differences, but they only mitigate, rather than destroy, the principle of the McCarran-Walter measure. It was not conviction, but political expediency, that led these senators to make this concession to a principle which they

[51] *Ibid.*, 455.

[52] S. 2842, 82d Cong., 2d sess., secs. 201, 203A.

considered "harsh and discriminatory."[53] Congress, however, rejected the substitute bill and enacted the McCarran-Walter bill over President Truman's veto.[54]

The President's veto message condemned the national origins system in language that attempted to recall to members of Congress and to Americans generally fundamental principles of the American creed of equality and freedom. The President stated that while a numerical limitation on immigration, consonant with our capacity to absorb, is needed, the national origins quota pattern "is insulting to large numbers of our finest citizens, irritating to our Allies abroad, and foreign to our purposes and ideals."

The national origins system, the President stated, "discriminates deliberately and intentionally, against many of the peoples of the world." The idea behind the quota policy, he said,

> was, to put it baldly, that Americans with English or Irish names were better people and better citizens than Americans with Italian or Greek or Polish names. It was thought that people of West European origin made better citizens than Rumanians or Yugoslavs or Ukranians or Balts or Austrians. Such a concept is utterly unworthy of our traditions and our ideals. It violates the great political doctrine of the Declaration of Independence

[53] Senator Herbert H. Lehman, *New York Times,* May 22, 1952.

[54] The Senate rejected the substitute for the McCarran bill by a vote of 51 to 27 on May 21, 1952. Following the defeat of this measure, the Senate, on May 22, 1952, passed with a voice vote the McCarran bill. Only about a dozen senators were on the floor at the time, and the lack of a quorum (49 senators) was not challenged. *New York Times,* May 23, 1952. Previously, on April 25, 1952, the House of Representatives passed the companion Walter bill by a vote of 206 to 68. There were some differences between the bills (see Conference Report, H. R. Report 2096, 82d Cong., 2d sess., June 9, 1952); the final draft was passed by the House of Representatives on June 10, 1952, by a vote of 302 to 53; by the Senate on June 11, 1952, by a voice vote, with fewer than a score of senators on the floor. The measure was vetoed by President Truman on June 25, 1952. (President's message in *New York Times,* June 26, 1952; reprinted in Appendix.) The bill was enacted over the veto on June 26, 1952. The vote in the House of Representatives was 278 to 113, in the Senate 57 to 26.

that "all men are created equal." It denies the humanitarian creed inscribed beneath the Statue of Liberty proclaiming to all nations: "Give me your tired, your poor, your huddled masses yearning to breathe free."

It repudiates our basic religious concepts, our belief in the brotherhood of man, and in the words of St. Paul that "there is neither Jew nor Greek, there is neither bond nor free. . . ."

The basis of this quota system was false and unworthy in 1924. It is even worse now. At the present time this quota system keeps out the very people we want to bring in. It is incredible to me that, in this year of 1952, we should again be enacting into law a slur on the patriotism, the capacity and the decency of a large part of our citizenry.

President Truman pointed out that the United States had entered into the North Atlantic Treaty Alliance (NATO) with nations whom we had asked to join with Americans in protecting the peace of the world against "one of the most terrible threats mankind has ever faced." Yet through the McCarran-Walter measure we were saying to these people—Greeks, Italians, Turks: "You are less worthy to come to this country than Englishmen or Irishmen."

Furthermore, it is fantastic to protect ourselves against a flood of immigrants from eastern Europe, for the countries in that part of the world have fallen under the Communist yoke—"they are silenced, fenced off by barbed wire and mine fields." We do not need to be protected against them; "on the contrary we want to stretch out a helping hand, to save those who have managed to flee into Western Europe, to succor those who are brave enough to escape from barbarism, to welcome and restore them against the day when their countries will, as we hope, be free again." The message pointed out that while there are 138,000 Poles in exile, the Polish quota is only 6,500; while there are 23,000 Baltic refugees, the quota for the subjugated Baltic countries is

700; while there are 30,000 Rumanian refugees, "who have managed to escape the labor camps and the mass deportations of their Soviet masters," the quota for Rumania is 289. These are only a few examples "of the absurdity, the cruelty of carrying over into this year of 1952 the isolationist limitations of our 1924 law." In brief, the quota system, "based upon assumptions at variance with our American ideals," the President said,

is long since out of date and more than ever unrealistic in the face of present world conditions.... In no other realm of our national life are we so hampered and stultified by the dead hand of the past as we are in this field of immigration.... The time to shake off this dead weight of past mistakes is now. The time to develop a decent policy of immigration—a fitting instrument for our foreign policy and a true reflection of the ideals we stand for, at home and abroad—is now.

Congress did not agree with President Truman. The two-thirds majority required to pass the bill over the veto was met with seventeen votes to spare in the House of Representatives and one vote to spare in the Senate, with party lines shattered.[55]

The President was more than usually sanguine when he stated in his veto message that he was sure that "with a little more time and a little more discussion in this country the public conscience and the good sense of the American people will assert themselves, and we shall be in a position to enact an immigration and naturalization policy that will be fair to all." It is doubtful if, apart from some mild revisions, the Immigration and Nationality Act of 1952 will be changed, in its basic features, in the near future. It took some seventy years for Congress to eliminate the flagrantly racist features of our immigration policy, and even then the change, as we have seen, was accomplished grudgingly and

[55] *New York Times,* June 27 and 28, 1952.

without a sense of vindication of a principle of justice.[56] To eliminate the formula of national origins, and with it the sting of inferiority that is felt by all Americans except those of English, Irish, or German descent, and by the peoples of the rest of the world, except a few privileged nations, may take years, despite the fact that, as President Truman stated in his veto message,

> what we do in the field of immigration and naturalization is vital to the continued growth and internal development of the United States—to the economic and social strength of our country—which is the core of the defense of the free world. Our immigration policy is equally, if not more, important to the conduct of our foreign relations and to our responsibilities of moral leadership in the struggle for world peace.

An act of Congress that would be effective internally and based on the proposition that all Americans who are descendants of the English, Irish, or German nations are superior to those who are descended from other nations or peoples and are to receive special privileges would be clearly unconstitutional. The national origins immigration laws have not been open to constitutional challenge, though they are based on this proposition, because the Supreme Court has held that the power of Congress in the field of immigration is plenary and is not subject to judicial challenge. The Supreme Court has failed or refused to see that an immigration law can discriminate against American citizens by reason of their race or national origin as much as can a law obviously directed at domestic or internal policy. Seven states[57] have effective statutes that bar discrimination in employment practices by private employers; these acts

[56] See note 32 *supra*.

[57] New York, New Jersey, Massachusetts, Connecticut, Rhode Island, Washington, and Oregon. Four other states—Colorado, Wisconsin, Illinois, and New Mexico—have fair employment practice acts that are of doubtful or limited usefulness.

prohibit discrimination on account of a person's "national origin." Yet Congress openly encourages such discrimination by a law based on the proposition that Americans are of unequal value and dignity.

In a message to Congress in 1906 President Theodore Roosevelt said: "Whether they are Catholic or Protestant, Jew or Gentile; whether they come from England or Germany, Russia, Japan or Italy, matters nothing. All we have a right to question is a man's conduct."[58] To depart from this standard of personal, individual worth means to substitute pseudo science for a genuine American ideal. The Senate Committee on the Judiciary, defending the national origins formula, said that the formula has provided "a fixed and easily determinable method for controlling immigration which is not subject to the whims and caprice of administrative interpretation."[59] But the formula is itself an expression of whims and caprice—no less so than were the Chinese and Japanese exclusion acts. Such expressions of whims and caprice have an impact on the quality and temper of life in the United States, as well as in the rest of the world, the significance of which can hardly be exaggerated. They tend to feed feelings of prejudice against the Roman Catholics and Jews who are American citizens by marking Protestants who themselves, or whose ancestors, have come from Britain or Germany as more assimilable to American institutions and culture. They stigmatize hundreds of millions of persons throughout the world, without whose good will the United States would find itself standing practically alone in opposition to Communism and Soviet Russia, as men of lesser breed and undesirable, no matter what their personal qualifications for admission into the United States may be. Man for man, the personal qualifications of an Italian may

[58] Quoted in M. J. Kohler, *Immigration and Aliens in the U.S.* (1936), 85.
[59] *Op. cit. supra* note 28, p. 448.

be superior to those of an Englishman, yet the latter will have an opportunity to apply for a quota number out of an annual total of 65,361, while the former will need to apply for a quota number out of an annual total of 5,645.[60] This is an absurd and unjust position to be taken by a country which, more than any other country in the world, places an emphasis on self-reliance, personal enterprise, the capacity to become successful without benefit of titles of nobility and inherited wealth, a belief in the proposition that "all men are created equal." "We conceive of Americanism," said a distinguished witness at the hearings on the McCarran-Walter bill,

> as the spirit behind the welcome that America has traditionally extended to people of all races, all religions, all nationalities. Americanism is a tolerant way of life that was devised by men who differed from one another vastly in religion, race, background, education, and lineage, and who agreed to forget all these things and ask of a new neighbor not where he comes from but only what he can do and what is his spirit toward his fellow men.[61]

Immigration, the witness added, needs to be regulated, controlled. But the regulation, he went on to say, "is the regulation of an asset, not of a liability. It is the control of something which is of benefit to this country."[62]

From the standpoint of the civil liberties of American citizens—as well as from the standpoint of fundamental human rights[63]— the most offensive aspect of American immigration

[60] The population of Great Britain, including Northern Ireland, is 50,-500,000; that of Italy 46,500,000.

[61] Simon H. Rifkind, former U.S. District Court Judge, testifying on behalf of the American Jewish Committee, the American Jewish Congress, the Synagogue Council of America, the Jewish Labor Committee, the Anti-Defamation League of B'nai Brith, and other Jewish organizations. *Joint Hearings Before the Subcommittees of the Committees on the Judiciary*, 82d Cong., 1st sess., on S. 716, H.R. 2379, and H.R. 2816 (1951), 566.

[62] *Ibid.*, 567.

[63] Cf. Universal Declaration of Human Rights, adopted by General As-

policy and legislation today is the national origins quota formula. There may be ways of justifying the formula if one reasons from presuppositions other than those which are basic in a society dedicated to the attainment of a maximum of freedom and justice.

But even the national origins quotas have been given by Congress in a begrudging spirit—a spirit that adds insult to injury, that gives a crust with one hand and takes it back with the other. We shall look at this phase of the McCarran-Walter Act briefly.

Large portions of the quota are not used. For example, in 1946 the quota was 153,879; but only 29,095 quota immigrants were admitted. In 1947 the quota was 153,929; but only 70,701 quota immigrants were admitted. The number of quota immigrants since 1931 has varied from a low of 8,220 in 1933 to a high of 113,046 in 1949.[64] The percentage of quotas used from 1930 to 1949, for all countries, has varied from 7.6 per cent in 1945 to 73.4 per cent in 1949.[65] The reason the quotas are unused to so large a degree is that the peoples of northern and western Europe are not keen to leave their own countries and migrate to the United States. Thus, the quota for this part of Europe was used only 5.8 per cent in 1945, only 13 per cent in 1946, and 53.5 per cent (the highest since 1930) in 1948; while the quota for southern and eastern Europe has been used to a much larger

---

sembly of the United Nations Organization, December 10, 1948. The first clause of the Preamble is as follows: "Whereas recognition of the inherent dignity and of the equal and inalienable rights of all members of the human family is the foundation of freedom, justice and peace in the world." The rights and freedoms set forth in the Declaration are to be enjoyed without distinction as to "race, color, sex, language, religion, political or other opinion, national or social origin, property, birth or other status." Article 2.

[64] Table 5 in *op. cit. supra* note 28, p. 890.

[65] *Ibid.*, Table 6, p. 890.

extent: 1945, 16.1 per cent; 1946, 46.3 per cent; 1947, 89.6 per cent.[66]

The quota system, in its national origins features, thus has no relation whatsoever to immigration pressures. These quotas were established with an eye only on the assumed composition of the American people in 1920 and with complete indifference as to whether the countries to whom the quotas were assigned needed or wanted them.

It was because of this circumstance that Congress felt compelled to enact emergency legislation to admit displaced persons. Had our quota system been realistically set up, even if with only one eye on the sources of immigration (not with both eyes on an arbitrary formula), the emergency legislation would have been unnecessary. A total of 400,744 persons were admitted under the emergency legislation, the first boatload arriving October 30, 1948, and the last boatload July 21, 1952.[67] This legislation did not set aside the existing requirements of health, literacy, and other qualifications that applied to normal quota immigrants; its emergency aspect is found in the fact that it temporarily set aside the quota limitations. This "marked a momentous change in the rigidly maintained barriers against the admission of immigrants to this country."[68]

The change was only temporary and partial. It was limited to the life of the Displaced Persons Commission, which completed its regular program activities on June 30, 1952. It was partial, for the national origins quotas were not abolished for the displaced persons program; they were, in fact, to the extent of 50 per cent, mortgaged against future years.

[66] Table in *Hearings Before the President's Commission on Immigration and Naturalization*, p. 1893.

[67] *Memo to America: The DP Story: Final Report of the U.S. Displaced Persons Commission* (1952), pp. v, 347.

[68] *Ibid.*, 345.

Thus 50 per cent of Latvia's quota is mortgaged until the year 2274. Its normal quota of 235 has thus been cut in half for 322 years following the passage of the McCarran-Walter Act. Estonia's quota has been mortgaged until the year 2146, or for 194 years; Greece's quota, for 61 years; Hungary's for 33 years; Lithuania's, for 135 years; Poland's, for 48 years; Rumania's, for 52 years.[69] Thus our displaced persons or refugee immigration policy was only a begrudging concession to the dictates of humanity and was set up on a system of accounts that is normally associated with mercantile buying and selling. It is for this reason that while only 47.3 per cent of the quota for northern and western Europe was used in 1949, for southern and eastern Europe the percentage was 210.4; for Great Britain and Northern Ireland, for example, it was 35.8 per cent, for Poland it was 329 per cent.[70]

It was such circumstances that led Senators Lehman and Humphrey and their associates to provide in their substitute bill that all quota numbers available in any year which are not actually issued and utilized shall be assigned to a general quota pool and made available without reference to national origins, in accordance with the following schedule: 25 per cent of the pooled quota numbers shall be assigned to make possible family reunions—admission of close relatives of citizens and permanent alien residents; 25 per cent for persons who, because of their skills, are urgently needed in the United States, or who are likely to be of special benefit to the national economy, cultural interests, or welfare of the country; 25 per cent for refugees from persecution because of their religion or race, or because of their adherence

[69] *New York Times,* May 23, 1953; see also President Truman's message to Congress of March 24, 1952, calling for admission of more European refugees. *New York Times,* March 25, 1952. See *Hearings Before the President's Commission on Immigration and Naturalization,* table on p. 1900; *Whom Shall We Welcome,* table on p. 104.

[70] *Op. cit. supra* note 28, table 6, p. 890.

to democratic beliefs or their opposition to totalitarianism; and the remainder of the pooled unused quotas shall be used to meet special circumstances or cases of hardship, at the discretion of the Secretary of State.[71]

If the national origins quota system is to continue, which will probably be the case for some years—practical politics being what it is,[72] the system ought to be divorced from our refugee and displaced persons immigration program—a step recommended by President Truman[73]—and it ought to be made flexible, along the lines set forth in the bill offered as a substitute for the McCarran-Walter measure,[74] by allowing the pooling and use of the unused national quotas.

Another provision of the 1952 law further fences in the national quotas. It provides[75] that the first 50 per cent of a national quota shall be made available to quota immigrants, otherwise qualified,

> whose services are determined by the Attorney General to be needed urgently in the United States because of the high education, technical training, specialized experience or exceptional ability of such immigrants and to be substantially beneficial prospectively to the national economy, cultural interests, or welfare of the United States.[76]

Admission within the first 50 per cent of a national quota shall be for such specially qualified personnel and their accompanying families. The next 30 per cent of a national quota are available to qualified quota immigrants who are

[71] S. 2842, 82d Cong., 2d sess., sec. 203A.

[72] Cf. editorial, *New York Times,* January 2, 1953.

[73] See note 69 *supra* for President's message.

[74] See note 71 *supra.*

[75] Sec. 203 (a).

[76] It should be noted that under the 1924 act professors and ministers, together with their families, were admitted as nonquota immigrants. 8 U.S.C. 204. Under the 1952 act, however, ministers continue to enjoy this special status, while professors are admitted only as quota immigrants under sec. 203 (a). Provision regarding ministers is made in Sec. 101 (a) (27).

the parents of citizens of the United States. The remaining 20 per cent of the quotas are available to qualified quota immigrants who are the husbands or wives or the minor children of resident aliens.

To place so much emphasis on technological and vocational qualifications is to remove every vestige of humanitarianism from our immigration policy. We deserve small thanks from those who come here if they are admitted because we find that they are "urgently" needed, by reason of their training and experience, to advance our national interests. This is hardly immigration; it is the importation of special skills or know-how, not greatly different from the importation of coffee or rubber. It is hardly in the spirit of American ideals to disregard a man's character and promise and to look only at his education and the vocational opportunities he had the good fortune to enjoy. An alien's search for the more abundant life contributes to the enrichment of the community. Nor do we deserve much credit for allowing the entry, within quota limits, of parents of American citizens, or the wife or husband and the minor children of aliens who had been lawfully admitted for permanent residence. Not to admit such persons would be to make our immigration law totally barbarous.[77]

But even so, within the limits fixed by law, there is discrimination; for an American citizen can easily bring into the United States his British parents, while another Amer-

[77] See Felix S. Cohen, *Immigration and National Welfare* (1940). The 1924 act also provided for preferential treatment within national quotas: 50 per cent for parents or husbands of citizens, and, where the nationality quota is 300 or more, for skilled agricultural workers and their families; the remainder of the quota for the wives and minor children of alien residents. 8 U.S.C. 206.

Nonquota status is enjoyed under the 1952 act by the husband or wife and the minor child of an American citizen. Sec. 101 (a) (27). Under the previous law special status was enjoyed by the wife or husband and the unmarried minor child of an American citizen. 8 U.S.C. 204 (a).

ican citizen may not be allowed to bring over his Latvian or Polish parents. If the latter American citizen were to ask why this is so, the answer would need to be, if we are candid, that Congress believes that this country has enough persons of Latvian or Polish nationality, that we do not want more of them or the "likes of them." Is it possible to deny that the law favors one American citizen and discriminates against another in distributing the privilege to bring over one's parents[78] or that the law makes of many Americans second-class citizens?[79]

We have here, it seems, what Ethan Brand, one of Hawthorne's characters, called the "Unpardonable Sin," which is, he said, "the sin of an intellect that triumphed over the sense of brotherhood with man and reverence for God, and sacrificed everything to its own mighty claims!" An observer of our immigration policy might well be tempted to say what Hawthorne said of Ethan Brand:

> So much for the intellect! But where was the heart? That, indeed, had withered,—had contracted,—had hardened,—had perished! It had ceased to partake of the universal throb. He had lost his hold of the magnetic chain of humanity. He was no longer a brother-man, opening the chambers or the dungeons of our common nature by the key of holy sympathy, which give him a right to share in all its secrets; he was now a cold observer, looking on mankind as the subject of his experiment, and, at length, converting man and woman to be his puppets, and pulling the wires that moved them.[80]

[78] Immigration of parents is used here only as an example of a systematic and radical order of discrimination.

[79] In his presidential campaign General Eisenhower said in Boston with regard to the McCarran-Walter Act: "Only second-class Americanism tolerates second-class citizenship. It's time to get rid of both, and that includes rewriting the unfair provisions of the McCarran Immigration Act." *New York Times,* October 22, 1952.

[80] Nathaniel Hawthorne, *The Snow Image and Other Tales* (Riverside Ed. of Hawthorne's *Works*), 484 ff, 495.

EXCLUSION OF SUBVERSIVES: SUBSTANTIVE PROVISIONS SUMMARIZED

Until 1903 no person was excluded from the United States solely because he entertained unorthodox opinions. In that year Congress passed a law[81] which provided for the exclusion of anarchists, "or persons who believe in or advocate the overthrow by force or violence of the Government of the United States, or of all government, or of all forms of law, or the assassination of public officials." The act also excluded persons who are members of or affiliated with organizations entertaining or teaching the doctrines of anarchy. The act was adopted in the aftermath of the assassination of President William McKinley in the fall of 1901 by Leon Czolgosz, an anarchist terrorist. This marked the beginning of an important and permanent feature of American immigration policy. The first law on the subject fixed the pattern that has since been followed in legislation on this subject: belief or advocacy, and membership or affiliation, were the key concepts.

The immigration law of 1917[82] reaffirmed the policy formulated in the earlier enactment and added as subject to the ban persons who advocate or teach the unlawful destruction of property, and persons who are members of or affiliated with organizations which advocate or teach the unlawful destruction of property.

On October 25, 1917, the Bolshevik forces went into action in Moscow, and Lenin announced the triumph of "the workers' and peasants' revolutions."[83] In October of the following year[84] Congress reaffirmed its determination to bar from entry persons who believe in or advocate—or are mem-

[81] 32 Stat. 1213 (1903). [82] 39 Stat. 874 (1917).
[83] E. H. Carr, *The Bolshevik Revolution, 1917-1923* (1951), I, 98-99.
[84] October 16, 1918.

bers of or affiliated with organizations that teach—the overthrow of government by force or violence.[85] The act was amended in 1920 to enlarge the class of excludable subversives.[86] In 1939 the Supreme Court said that the act banned the admission of persons who "at entry"—i.e., at the time of entry—were members of or affiliated with a proscribed organization.[87] Congress in 1940 amended the act so that the prohibition on admission would apply to "any alien who, at any time, shall be or shall have been" a member of a proscribed class.[88]

As the law read after its amendment in 1940, the following persons were barred from admission into the United States: (a) anarchists; (b) aliens who are opposed to "all organized government"; (c) aliens who are advocates of the violent overthrow of the government of the United States, "or of all forms of law," or of the assassination of officers of the government of the United States "or of any other organized government," or of the destruction of property, or of sabotage. The ban applied to persons who believe in, advise, advocate, or teach, or who are members of or affiliated with organizations that believe in, advise, advocate, or teach these doctrines.[89] The ban also applied to aliens who write, publish, or who knowingly circulate, distribute, print, or display, or who cause these acts to be done, or have in their possession for the purpose of circulation, distribution, publication, or display, any written or

[85] 40 Stat. 1012 (1918). [86] 41 Stat. 1008 (1920).

[87] Kessler v. Strecker, 307 U.S. 22 (1939). The case involved deportation, but the court construed the language of the act in such a way that the decision was taken to apply to admissions as well.

[88] 54 Stat. 673 (1940).

[89] As to group (b) in the text, the statute did not use the term "believe in," but only "advise, advocate, or teach." All four terms—believe, advise, advocate, and teach—are used with regard to group (c). There is also a ban on polygamists and advocates of polygamy. 8 U.S.C. 136 (f); sec. 212 (a) (11) of the 1952 act.

printed matter which advises, advocates, or teaches any of the proscribed doctrines, or who are members of or affiliated with any group or organization that does any of these acts. Financial assistance to a group or organization constitutes affiliation; and giving, loaning, or promising money to be used for teaching, advising, or advocacy is itself teaching, advising or advocacy.[90]

The Subversive Activities Control Act of 1950[91] made some important additions to the law. It banned the admission of aliens who seek to enter the United States solely, principally, or incidentally to engage in activities "which would be prejudicial to the public interest, or would endanger the welfare or safety of the United States."[92] This is probably as broad a provision as could be devised. The act also added the following significant provision: the exclusion of aliens who are members of or affiliated with the Communist party of the United States, or any other totalitarian party of the United States, or of any state, or of any foreign country, or of any affiliate or subdivision of any such party.[93] This was the first time Congress expressly named the Communist party in any immigration statute. The 1950 act also banned the entry of aliens who advocate "the economic, international, and governmental doctrines of world communism or the economic and governmental doctrines of any other form of totalitarianism," or who are members of or affiliated with any organization that advocates these doctrines. The act also excluded aliens about whom "there is reason to believe" that after entry they would be likely to

[90] 8 U.S.C. 137.

[91] Pub. Law 831, 81st Cong., 2d sess., ch. 1024, being Title I of the Internal Security Act of 1950.

[92] Sec. 22. An earlier act, 62 Stat. 635 (1948), also banned the entry of aliens who seek to come into the United States in order to engage in activities that will endanger the public safety.

[93] The act applies also to any predecessors or successors of such party regardless of name.

engage in activity "subversive to the national security" or in any activity a purpose of which is the opposition to, or the control or overthrow of, the government of the United States by force, violence, "or other unconstitutional means."

The McCarran-Walter Act of 1952 in an omnibus fashion took over all the previously enacted statutes and made several additions to the law:

(1) The 1950 act, as we have seen, banned the entry af aliens who advocate "the economic, international, and governmental doctrines of world communism or the economic and governmental doctrines of any other form of totalitarianism," or who are members of or affiliated with any organization that advocates these doctrines. The 1952 act bans the admission of aliens who advocate the economic, international, and governmental doctrines of world communism, "or the establishment *in the United States* of a totalitarian dictatorship," or who are members of or affiliated with any organization that advocates these doctrines.[94]

(2) Soon after the 1950 act went into effect noted literary figures, like Graham Greene, and scientists, like Marcus Oliphant and Ernest B. Chain, met great difficulties when they attempted to enter the United States for temporary visits. These experiences have been thus summarized:

> In the past few years a very large number of distinguished European scientists, almost all of them anti-Communists and deeply devoted to the freedom in which scientific truth is sought and discovered, have been frustrated in their efforts to come to the United States to share their knowledge with their American colleagues. Their applications for visas have in many cases been refused, usually after long delay; in other cases the visas have been finally granted, but only after delays so long that the scientific meetings to which they were invited had taken place, or the teaching appointments for which they had been engaged

[94] Sec. 212 (a) (28) (D). Italics added. Also sec. 212 (a) (28) (G).

had lapsed through their failure to arrive in time to fulfill them. In still other cases the applicants have received no decision whatsoever from the American consular officers to whom they applied.[95]

On March 28, 1951, Congress amended the law[96] to permit entry if former membership in proscribed organizations was involuntary; the amendment lifted the barrier for aliens who had joined such organizations when they were less than sixteen years old, when they were forced to join by law, or when membership was essential to secure work or food. The 1952 act carries over essentially the same provision.[97] The statute provides that a visa may be issued if the consular officer finds that (1) the membership or affiliation was involuntary, or obtained only while the applicant was under sixteen years of age, by operation of law, or was for the purpose of obtaining employment, food rations, or other essentials of living "and where necessary for such purposes," or (2) since termination of the membership or affiliation the alien has been, for at least five years prior to the date of his application, "actively opposed to the doctrine, program, principles, and ideology" of the party or organization, *and* that his admission into the United States would be in the public interest.

If the alien is given a visa by a consular officer under the above provision of the act, the alien may be admitted only if he establishes "to the satisfaction of the Attorney General," and if the Attorney General finds, all of the elements in the case required by the act. If the admission is allowed

[95] E. A. Shils, "America's Paper Curtain," editorial in 8 *Bulletin of the Atomic Scientists* (October 1952), 210. The entire issue is devoted to the theme "American Visa Policy and Foreign Scientists."

[96] Act of March 28, 1951, ch. 23, Pub. Law 14, 82d Cong., 1st sess. See Harris, "McCarran's Iron Curtain," *New Republic* (March 3, 1952), 12.

[97] Sec. 212 (a) (28) (I). These changes were adopted without an eye on the problem of the scientist or scholar and have hardly affected this problem. See Appendix IV.

under the conditions required for case (2) in the preceding paragraph, the Attorney General is required to make promptly a detailed report to Congress in the case of each alien thus admitted.

In tracing the development of congressional policy, as we have done, it becomes apparent that the most important changes in the law were enacted in 1950, in the Subversive Activities Control Act (also known as the McCarran Act) and were incorporated in the Immigration and Nationality Act of 1952 (the McCarran-Walter Act).

PROCEDURAL PROVISIONS

As we have seen in our discussion of the quota provisions of the law, it is virtually impossible for an alien seriously to contemplate his admission to the United States as an immigrant unless it can be shown that he fits into one of the statutory preferred classes or is a nonquota immigrant, e.g., that he is the minor child or parent of an American citizen. The law provides that the proceedings are to be initiated by the American citizen, who is required to file a petition with the Attorney General. The regulations adopted under the act provide the form, the information, and the documentary proofs with which the applicant needs to comply. After an investigation of the facts, the Attorney General, if he finds that the facts stated are true and that the alien for whom the petition was made is eligible for admission, approves the petition and forwards a copy to the Department of State. The Secretary of State then authorizes the consular officer concerned to grant the nonquota, quota, or preference status. The act provides, however, that the grant of such status shall not entitle the alien to admission if upon his arrival at a port of entry he is found not to be entitled to such classification.[98] Also, the Attorney General may "at any

[98] Sec. 205.

time, for what he deems to be good and sufficient cause," revoke the approval of a petition that had been approved by him.[99] The procedure discussed up to this point is concerned only with the determination of the alien's classification within the quota scheme.

The immigrant also needs to meet the following requirements: (1) He must have a valid immigrant visa. (2) He must be properly chargeable to the quota specified in the visa, or be a nonquota immigrant. (3) He must have the proper status under the quota. (4) He must be otherwise admissible under the act.[100] (Of course, if the total number of immigrant visas under the same quota has already been issued, the immigrant cannot gain admission.[101])

There are detailed provisions for the issuance of visas by consular officers. The alien who applies for a visa is registered and fingerprinted; he is required to take a physical and mental examination. No visa is issued if the consular officer "*knows or has reason to believe*" that the alien is ineligible under any provision of law.[102] After the issuance of a visa, the consular officer or the Secretary of State "may at any time, in his discretion, revoke such visa or other documentation."[103] Furthermore, possession of a visa does not entitle the alien to entry if at the port of entry he is found to be inadmissible by the Attorney General.

When an alien applies for a visa he is required to furnish information concerning himself, his past, his future intentions, his close relatives, and such additional information as may be necessary to the enforcement of the Immigration and Nationality Act. He must present a passport or other

[99] Sec. 206. If the notice of revocation is not communicated to the alien before he commences his journey, then his admissibility is to be determined in the manner provided by other parts of the act; namely, secs. 235 and 236. These sections will be summarized later.

[100] Sec. 211. [101] Sec. 211 (d).

[102] Sec. 221 (g). Italics added. [103] Sec. 221 (i).

suitable travel document, certified copies of his record of birth, and military and other records.

As can be readily seen from what has been said thus far, a great deal of discretion is vested in the consular officers of foreign countries and in the Attorney General. There are additional provisions along the same line. An alien is not to be admitted if the consular officer or the Attorney General is of the opinion that he is "likely at any time" to become a public charge;[104] or if the consular officer or the Attorney General "*knows or has reason to believe*" that he seeks to enter "solely, principally, or incidentally to engage in activities which would be prejudicial to the public interest, or endanger the welfare, safety, or security of the United States."[105]

With regard to aliens who have been members of or affiliated with proscribed organizations, a visa may nonetheless be issued, as we have noted, if the alien establishes "to the satisfaction of the consular officer" that (a) the membership or affiliation was involuntary or obtained solely when the alien was under sixteen years of age, by operation of law, or for purposes of obtaining employment, food rations, or other essentials of living, and if membership or affiliation was necessary for such purposes; or that (b) since the termination of the membership or affiliation the alien has been, for at least five years preceding the application for a visa, actively opposed to the doctrine, program, principles, and ideology of the organization, *and* that the admission of the alien into the United States "would be in the public interest." If the visa is issued under these circumstances, the alien must apply for admission to the United States, and must then establish the same facts "to the satisfaction of the Attorney General." When an alien is admitted under circumstances described in (b) above, the Attorney General is re-

[104] Sec. 212 (a) (15). [105] Sec. 212 (a) (27).

quired to make promptly a detailed report of the case to Congress.[106]

Aliens are not to be admitted if the consular officer or the Attorney General "knows or has reasonable ground to believe" that they "probably would" after entry engage in activities subversive to the national security; or in any activity a purpose of which is opposition to the government of the United States, or its control or overthrow, by force, violence or other unconstitutional means; or join, affiliate, or participate in the activities of a proscribed organization.[107]

Assuming that an alien meets all the conditions described up to this point, and arrives at an American port of entry, and has in his possession a visa and other documents required by law, he must be ready to meet and satisfy other statutory requirements.

A physical and mental examination is made by medical officers of the United States Public Health Service. Then immigration officers conduct an examination under regulations prescribed by the Attorney General. One phase of the examination is to determine whether the alien belongs to any of the excluded classes.[108] An alien "who may not appear to the examining immigration officer at the port of arrival to be *clearly and beyond a doubt* entitled to land" shall be

[106] Sec. 212 (a) (28) (I).

[107] Sec. 212 (a) (29). It should be noted here that upon recommendation by the Secretary of State or the consular officer and the approval by the Attorney General a nonimmigrant visa for a temporary visit may be granted to an alien who is ineligible unless his ineligibility is determined under the provisions of the law cited in this footnote and in footnote 105 *supra*. If he does permit a temporary entry, the Attorney General must make a detailed report on the case to Congress. The Attorney General also has the power at his discretion to parole an alien into the United States temporarily under such conditions as he may prescribe for "emergent [sic] reasons or for reasons deemed strictly in the public interest." Sec. 212 (d) (5).

[108] Sec. 235 (a). The new regulations adopted under the 1952 act were published in 17 *Federal Register* (December 19, 1952), 11469-11564.

detained for further inquiry by a special inquiry officer.[109] If the decision of the examining immigration officer is, however, favorable to the alien, the decision is subject to challenge by any other immigration officer, and then the question of his admission or exclusion goes to a special inquiry officer.

If an alien appears to the examining immigration officer or to the special inquiry officer to be excludable because of his subversive beliefs, membership or affiliation, past or present,[110] or because he may engage in activities which would be prejudicial to the public interest[111] or subversive to the national security,[112] his case is reported to the Attorney General. If the Attorney General is satisfied that the alien is excludable

> on the basis of information of a confidential nature, the disclosure of which the Attorney General, in the exercise of his discretion, and after consultation with the appropriate security agencies of the Government, concludes would be prejudicial to the public interest, safety, or security, he may in his discretion order such alien to be excluded and deported without any inquiry or further inquiry by a special inquiry officer.[113]

In a case in which the examining immigration officer does not admit the alien, and the matter is not referred to the Attorney General directly, the matter is then presented to a special inquiry officer. This officer examines the alien and his evidence. He has the authority to determine whether the alien shall be allowed to enter or shall be excluded, or whether the matter shall be referred to the Attorney General under the circumstances discussed in the preceding paragraph. His determination shall be based "only on the evi-

[109] Sec. 235 (b). Italics added.
[110] Under sec. 212 (a) (28).
[111] Under sec. 212 (a) (27).
[112] Under sec. 212 (a) (29).
[113] Sec. 235 (c).

dence produced at the inquiry." He may not conduct the proceedings if he had participated in the case in its earlier stages as an investigating or prosecuting official. The procedure before him shall be in accordance with the provisions of the Immigration and Nationality Act of 1952 and the regulations of the Attorney General.[114] The inquiry is to "be kept separate and apart from the public." The alien may have "one friend or relative" present, under such conditions as may be prescribed by the Attorney General;[115] but he shall have the privilege of being represented by counsel of his own choice.[116] A complete record of all testimony and evidence produced at the inquiry shall be kept.[117] If the special inquiry officer decides against the alien, the latter may appeal to the Attorney General; if he decides in favor of the alien, the immigration officer may take such an appeal. The decision of the Attorney General shall be rendered solely upon the evidence produced before the special inquiry officer, except in a case where the Attorney General is satisfied that the alien should be excluded on the basis of information of a confidential nature.[118] The decision of a special inquiry officer to exclude an alien is final unless reversed on appeal by the Attorney General.[119]

When a person applies for a visa or makes application for admission, the burden of proof is upon him to establish his eligibility, or that he is not subject to exclusion, or that he is entitled to any specific status under the quota provisions. If he fails to establish his eligibility "to the satisfaction of

[114] Sec. 236 (a) excludes application of the Administrative Procedure Act of 1946, 5 U.S.C. 1001.

[115] Sec. 236 (a).

[116] Sec. 292. This privilege extends to any exclusion or deportation proceeding before a special inquiry officer and any appeal before the Attorney General from any exclusion or deportation proceeding.

[117] Sec. 236 (a). [118] Secs. 236 (b) and 235 (c).

[119] Sec. 236 (c).

the consular officer," no visa or other document required for entry shall be issued to him. An alien shall not be admitted to the United States unless he establishes "to the satisfaction of the Attorney General" that he is not subject to exclusion under any provision of the law.[120]

QUESTION OF CONSTITUTIONALITY

As we have seen from our discussion at the beginning of this chapter, the Supreme Court has held that the power of Congress with regard to admissions and exclusions of immigrants is plenary; this power is not limited in any way by the Bill of Rights.

At this point we shall look at the question of constitutionality with an eye, first, on the relevance of the First Amendment guarantees of freedom of speech, press, and assembly, and freedom of religion; and, second, on the relevance of the procedural due process guarantee of the Fifth Amendment.

Substantive Provisions

It will be recalled that in 1903 Congress, for the first time, enacted legislation to exclude aliens because of their beliefs.[121] The act provided for the exclusion and deportation of "anarchists, or persons who believe in or advocate the overthrow by force or violence of the Government of the United States, or of all government, or of all forms of law." The act was passed in March. In October of the same year John Turner, a British anarchist, was detained for deportation. He had entered the United States surreptitiously ten days before the warrant of arrest was issued. Throughout the discussion by the Supreme Court, the case was treated as one of exclusion, on the theory, I suppose, that the pres-

[120] Sec. 291. [121] 32 Stat. 1313 (1903).

ence for a brief period of time of an excludable alien does not make him a resident alien,[122] so that his case may be treated as one of exclusion rather than of deportation.

During the ten days he was at liberty, Turner had delivered a lecture in New York in which he declared himself to be an anarchist. In this lecture he apparently urged the use and efficacy of a general strike. His attorneys, Edgar L. Masters and Clarence Darrow, however, denied that he was an anarchist within the meaning of the statute, arguing that he was not an *advocate* of anarchism but was only a philosophical anarchist, who "regarded the absence of government as a political ideal." They contended that the 1903 statute was unconstitutional because it was a law that abridged freedom of speech and press, and it was beyond the competency of Congress to pass a bill of this description. The fact that aliens are the subject of the prohibition or abridgement, they maintained, was of no moment, since Congress is incompetent to pass *any* law that prohibits or abridges speech. They also challenged the view that Congress may exclude aliens because it has the powers inherent in any sovereign government or nation; Congress, they maintained, has only delegated powers, defined by the Constitution and subject to constitutional limitations, and no power, they argued, "is delegated by the Constitution to general government over alien friends with reference to their admission into the United States or otherwise, or over the beliefs of citizens, denizens, sojourners, or aliens, or over the freedom of speech or of the press."

The court, in an opinion by Chief Justice Fuller, rebuffed all these contentions. Congress, said the court, has the power to exclude aliens; to prescribe the terms and conditions on which they may enter; and to deport aliens who

[122] Louis B. Boudin, "The Settler Within Our Gates," 26 *N.Y.U. Law Rev.* (1951), 266, 451, 634, at pp. 287-290.

have entered in violation of law. These powers, said the court, are no longer open to constitutional objection, whether they be rested (a) on the principle of international law that every sovereign nation has the power, "inherent in sovereignty and essential to self-preservation," to exclude aliens, or to admit them "only in such cases and upon such conditions as it may see fit to prescribe"; or (b) on the constitutional power to regulate commerce with foreign nations. Chief Justice Fuller quoted with approval from an earlier opinion of the court: "No limits can be put by the courts upon the power of Congress to protect . . . the country from the advent of aliens whose race or habits render them undesirable as citizens, or to expel such if they have already found their way into our land, and unlawfully remain therein."

With respect to the contention that the statute violates the guarantees of the First Amendment, the court said: "We are at a loss to understand in what way the act is obnoxious to this objection." It is, of course, true that an alien who is excluded or expelled is cut off from publishing or speaking in this country, "but that is merely because of his exclusion therefrom"; but "those who are excluded cannot assert the rights in general obtaining in a land to which they do not belong as citizens or otherwise."

With respect to the contention that the statute should not apply to philosophical anarchists, who are "merely political philosophers, whose teachings are beneficial rather than otherwise," and whose views are "innocent of evil intent," the court held that such persons may be excluded if "Congress was of the opinion that the tendency of the general exploitation of such views is so dangerous to the public weal that aliens who hold and advocate them would be undesirable additions to our population, whether permanently or temporarily, whether many or few." As long as governments endure, said Chief Justice Fuller, "they cannot be denied the power of self-preservation."[123]

The court spoke of the government's power of self-preservation. This might imply that the proscribed doctrines are only such as advocate the destruction of the government or of all government. But the decision cannot, I think, be read so narrowly. Advocacy of polygamy, for example, would not threaten the existence of the government; yet it is not doubted today that Congress may exclude (as it does) aliens who advocate polygamy.[124] All other doctrines the advocacy of which are proscribed in the 1952 statute may be said to be such as would threaten the existence of such government as the United States Constitution contemplates. If an alien who advocates the practice of polygamy were barred from entry and his case were to reach the Supreme Court, it is highly probable that the court would expand the *ratio decidendi* of the *Turner* case and hold that Congress may exclude from the United States aliens who advocate the destruction of the government or of an essential element of American civilization.[125]

Suppose Congress were to amend the act of 1952 so that persons who advocate or teach the doctrine that religion is

[123] Mr. Justice Brewer wrote a separate opinion in which he said that the facts seemed to show that Turner was an anarchist in the sense that he urged and sought the overthrow by force of all government. If he were only a philosophical anarchist, he should have shown this to be the fact. It was unnecessary, therefore, to consider what rights he would have if he had shown that he was only a philosophical anarchist. The clear implication is that all nine Justices agreed that the exclusion or deportation of aliens who advocate a proscribed doctrine is constitutional.

Brewer also commented on the argument of inherent powers, but by way of dissent, as a *caveat*. Congress, he said, "is not authorized in all things to act for the nation," and too little effect has been given to the Tenth Amendment. The powers not named in the Constitution, either expressly or by implication, "are reserved to the people, and can be exercised only by them, or upon further grant from them."

[124] Sec. 212 (2) (11) of the act of 1952.

[125] Cf. Davis v. Beason, 133 U.S. 333 (1890); Reynolds v. U.S., 98 U.S., 145 (1879).

superstition or is "the opium of the people"[126] shall be barred from entry. The court would sustain the act probably on the group libel theory, saying that if a state may prohibit publications which expose any race to contempt or which are productive of breaches of the peace or of riot, or which are lewd and obscene, or which are "fighting words,"[127] Congress may refuse admission to persons who would commit these or similar offenses.

Suppose Congress were to become impressed with the argument one sometimes hears these days that the Catholic population, unless retarded in the future, will increase to the point where Catholics will be the predominant religious denomination,[128] or the argument that Jews constitute a pressure group,[129] and as a consequence were to prohibit the admission of Catholics or Jews.[130] In such an instance the Supreme Court would still be able to uphold the act, on the grounds urged by the attorney for the government in the

[126] Karl Marx, *A Criticism of the Hegelian Philosophy of Law* (1844).

[127] Beauharnais v. Ill., 72 S. Ct. 725 (1952).

[128] For figures, see Anson Phelps Stokes, *Church and State in the U.S.* (1950), I, 56 ff.

[129] Of all the immigrants under the Displaced Persons Act, 47 per cent were Catholic and 16 per cent were Jews, or a total of 63 per cent were persons of the Roman Catholic and Jewish faiths. *Memo to America: the DP Story, Final Report of U.S. Displaced Persons Commission* (1952), 248. (This percentage was lower than the ratio of Catholics and Jews in DP status abroad.) Apparently with these figures in mind, Representative Francis E. Walter, co-sponsor of the Immigration and Nationality Act of 1952, in attacking the report of the President's Commission on Immigration and Naturalization, said that the Commission, in planning its report, "started out by corralling certain professional social workers who have helped in bringing to the United States over 400,000 displaced persons and who are understandingly eager to continue their jobs." *New York Times*, January 10, 1953; *Cong. Rec.*, January 9, 1952, p. 316 (daily ed.). He also spoke of "professional Jews." *Cong. Rec.*, January 13, 1952, p. 380 (daily ed.).

[130] This is offered as an extreme case for discussion purposes only. The author rejects the inference that he believes a majority of the members of Congress to be capable of acting in such a flagrantly discriminatory fashion; no doubt, *some* members of Congress would, if given an opportunity, act out their beliefs in the doctrines of white supremacy and Protestant (of course *their* private brand of Protestant) rule.

Turner case; namely, "The right to exclude or to expel all aliens, or any class of aliens, absolutely or upon certain conditions, in war or in peace, is an inherent and inalienable right of every sovereign, independent nation, essential to its safety, its independence, and its welfare."[131] This is in effect the "political question" doctrine; namely, that questions in their nature "political" can be answered only by Congress or by the President and are beyond the scope of the judicial power for review.[132] From this position it is apparent that the national origins formula, racial or religious exclusion, and any other substantive aspect of American immigration policy are beyond judicial challenge.

The Supreme Court could have taken, and still can take—though the probability that it will is extremely remote—another line of thought. From the standpoint of what is in the Constitution, the power to deport does not enjoy greater clarity and certainty than does the power to exclude aliens; as a matter of fact, as we shall see in the next chapter, the power to deport was originally only an incident or adjunct of the power to exclude. Yet when the Supreme Court asserted the proposition that the deportation power is inherent in American sovereignty and is not, therefore, subject to constitutional limitations, Mr. Justice Brewer wrote a strong dissent. "The governments of other nations have elastic powers," he said. "Ours are fixed by a written constitution." History shows that despotic governments have expelled peoples because of their race or religion, but the Constitution of the United States, framed by men well acquainted with the lessons of history, delegated no such power to the gov-

[131] See report of case in 48 Law. Ed. 979, at 983. In support of this proposition were cited Fong Yue Ting v. U.S., 149 U.S. 711 (1893); Chinese Exclusion Cases, 130 U.S. 581 (1889); Nishimura Ekiu v. U.S., 142 U.S. 651 (1891).

[132] See Fong Yue Ting v. U.S. and Nishimura Ekiu v. U.S., cited *supra* note 131.

ernment.[133] The force of this argument can be felt by the power to exclude no less than by the power to expel. These powers are of equal constitutional dignity or equally subject to constitutional attack. But the argument has not been made by any member of the Supreme Court, nor is it likely to be made. In a case decided in 1952, Mr. Justice Jackson said for a majority of the court: "We think that, in the present state of the world, it would be rash and irresponsible to reinterpret our fundamental law to deny or qualify the Government's power of deportation."[134] There can be little if any doubt that the court would take a different position with regard to the admissions and exclusions policies in immigration law.

It is interesting to see to what length the court has gone to immunize from constitutional attack the power of Congress in the field of immigration policy. As we have seen, Mr. Justice Murphy has said that the Bill of Rights is beyond the reach of an alien seeking admission into the United States.[135] Yet he also said, in another case, that even a state of war does not suspend the Bill of Rights.[136] Certainly the power to wage war may be no less necessary for national survival than is the power to regulate immigration; yet the war powers, expressly delegated to Congress and the President, were, in the mind of Mr. Justice Murphy, subject to constitutional limitations, while the power to admit or exclude aliens, at the most an implied power, was free from such restraints.

This discussion of the constitutional aspects of the sub-

[133] Fong Yue Ting v. U.S., cited *supra* note 131.

[134] Harisiades v. Shaughnessy, 342 U.S. 580 (1952). Justices Black and Douglas dissented; Justice Clark did not participate in the case.

[135] Case cited *supra* note 6.

[136] Conc. op. in Hirabayashi v. U.S., 320 U.S. 81 (1943). "Congress and the President, like the courts, possess no power not derived from the Constitution." Ex parte Quirin, 317 U.S. 1 (1942). Cf. dissent of Justices Murphy and Rutledge, In re Yamashita, 327 U.S. 1 (1946).

stantive provisions of our immigration law points up the wisdom of Mr. Justice Frankfurter's observation that reliance for the most precious interests of civilization must be found outside of their vindication in our courts: "Only a persistent positive translation of the faith of a free society into the convictions and habits and actions of a community is the ultimate reliance against unabated temptations to fetter the human spirit."

Procedural Due Process

Our discussion discloses the impossibility of a constitutional attack on the substantive provisions of our immigration law. Now we shall consider briefly the constitutional question with regard to the procedural aspects of the exclusion of aliens. This topic can be best introduced and summarized by a discussion of the *Ellen Knauff* case,[137] decided by the Supreme Court in 1950.

Ellen Knauff was born in Germany in 1915. During the Hitler regime she went to Czechoslovakia. In 1939 she went to England as a refugee, and while there she served, for over three years, with the Royal Air Force "efficiently and honorably." Then she secured civilian employment with the War Department of the United States in Germany, where her work was rated "very good" and "excellent." With permission of the Commanding General at Frankfurt, she married in 1948 Kurt Knauff, a naturalized American citizen and an American Army veteran of World War II, who was at the time of the marriage a civilian employee of the American Army at Frankfurt.

In August 1948 Mrs. Knauff, proceeding under the provi-

[137] U.S. ex. rel. Knauff v. Shaughnessy, 338 U.S. 537 (1950). The decision was 4 to 3, with Justices Frankfurter, Black, and Jackson dissenting. Justices Douglas and Clark did not participate. The opinion for the majority was by Justice Minton.

sions of the War Brides Act,[138] sought to enter the United States to be naturalized. She was detained at Ellis Island for about two months, and then the Assistant Commissioner of Immigration and Naturalization recommended that she be permanently excluded *without a hearing* on the ground that her admission would be prejudicial to the interests of the United States. On the same day on which this recommendation was made, the Attorney General adopted the recommendation and made a final order of exclusion. Mrs. Knauff then instituted *habeas corpus* proceedings to test the legality of her detention and exclusion. The United States District Court dismissed the writ; this action was sustained by the Court of Appeals, and then affirmed by the Supreme Court.

It was the contention of Mrs. Knauff that her exclusion without a hearing was in violation of (1) the statutes of Congress and of (2) the due process clause of the Fifth Amendment.

With regard to (1), the Supreme Court found that the Attorney General had exercised the discretion entrusted to him by an act of Congress of 1941 and a proclamation by the President issued pursuant to this act. The Attorney General had, therefore, the statutory right to exclude Mrs. Knauff on the basis of confidential information and without giving her an opportunity to be heard.

With regard to (2), Mr. Justice Minton disposed of this matter with the succinct sentence: "Whatever the procedure authorized by Congress is, it is due process so far as a denied entry is concerned." Mrs. Knauff got the treatment that Congress had authorized; she had, therefore, no cause for complaint—that is, in so far as the Constitution is concerned. If Congress provides for summary exclusion, the alien knocking at our gates—even if she is the war bride of a man

[138] 59 Stat. 659, ch. 591 (1945); 8 U.S.C. 232.

who is a citizen and a veteran—may be barred without a hearing.

Three Justices of the Supreme Court dissented; but no member of the court raised any question respecting the disposition of the constitutional issue; all agreed that an alien who seeks admission is entitled only to the procedure authorized by Congress; if the alien is treated in accordance with the statutory requirements, his treatment is "due process." That there may be a wide breach between the statutory procedure and what a standard of common justice and decency may require is shown by what happened to Mrs. Knauff after she lost the appeal in the Supreme Court.

The House of Representatives apparently was impressed with the dissenting opinions in the court. Mr. Justice Frankfurter said of the majority's opinion: "This is not the way to read such legislation." Congress, he said, intended to give a bounty to the member of the armed forces who had honorably served his country; yet, he said, the effect of the decision is

> that the deepest tie that an American soldier could form may be secretly severed on the mere say-so of an official, however well intentioned. Although five minutes of cross examination could enable the soldier-husband to dissipate seemingly convincing information affecting the security danger of his wife, that opportunity need not be accorded. All of this, because of the literal reading of the provision of the War Brides Act . . . It is true also of Acts of Congress that "the letter killeth." Legislation should not be read in such a decimating spirit unless the letter of Congress is inexorable.

Mr. Justice Jackson[139] also found that Congress had not authorized "an abrupt and brutal exclusion of the wife of an American citizen without a hearing." Congress, he said,

[139] Justices Frankfurter and Black joined Justice Jackson in his dissenting opinion.

will have to use more explicit language than any yet cited before I will agree that it has authorized an administrative officer to break up the family of an American citizen or force him to keep his wife by becoming an exile. Likewise, it will have to be much more explicit before I can agree that it authorized a finding of serious misconduct against the wife of an American citizen without notice of charges, evidence of guilt and a chance to meet it.[140]

Four months after the court decided the case, the House of Representatives passed a special bill to permit Mrs. Knauff to enter the United States and to become a citizen.[141] The subcommittee of the Committee on the Judiciary of the Senate failed, however, to act upon the bill. Because of public interest and concern, the Board of Immigration Appeals afforded Mrs. Knauff a hearing early in 1951. Her right to enter was, however, denied, and she was ordered deported. Mr. Justice Jackson stayed the order. Six months later the Board of Immigration Appeals reversed itself and recommended her admission. On the very next day the Attorney General adopted this recommendation and Mrs. Knauff was admitted to the United States. She had been detained by the immigration authorities for about three years.[142]

Mrs. Knauff's exclusion came before the courts in a *habeas corpus* proceeding. It should be pointed out that review of an order of exclusion is always available to an alien in such a proceeding. This is true today as it was in 1950. But the scope of the review is strictly limited, as we have seen in the *Knauff* case, to the question whether the immigration offi-

[140] As we have noted, no member of the court questioned the constitutionality of a summary exclusion of an alien. Justice Jackson said: "I do not question the constitutional power of Congress to authorize immigration authorities to turn back from our gates any alien or class of aliens."

[141] The Supreme Court decided the case January 16, 1950; the bill was passed May 2, 1950.

[142] *New York Times,* November 2 and 3, 1951. Mrs. Knauff has herself told the story in *The Ellen Knauff Story* (1952).

cers and the Attorney General have exceeded the authority vested in them by Congress. Such officials must act within the confines of their delegated authority; they must exercise their discretion within the statutory bounds and according to the forms fixed by law. The courts will, therefore, in a *habeas corpus* proceeding examine the record to see if the officers have performed their acts in accordance with the law. But if Congress vests final authority in an administrative officer, and gives no right to the courts to review his findings and conclusions, the officer becomes exclusive judge, and no court will review, let alone reverse, his decision. Thus, the provision in the act of 1952 which gives the Attorney General the power to exclude an alien "on the basis of information of a confidential nature,"[143] means that in a *habeas corpus* proceeding to test the legality of an exclusion under this provision the court will not have before it the facts on the basis of which the Attorney General made his order of exclusion. The only question for the court's consideration will be whether it was the Attorney General (and not the Postmaster General) who made the final order.

The alien, when he reaches an American port of entry, lives under a government of men, not under a government of laws, in so far as Congress has subjected the alien to the absolute discretion of certain officers. The alien can find practically no protection in the Constitution. The case of Ellen Knauff has settled this question.[144]

[143] Sec. 235 (c).

[144] As we have seen, there was no dissent in the Supreme Court from the decision on this point.

On March 16, 1953, the Supreme Court decided the case of Shaughnessy v. United States ex rel. Mezei, 73 S. Ct. 625, in which it was held that an alien may be detained on Ellis Island indefinitely without the Attorney General being required to disclose the grounds or evidence for his belief that the detained alien is a security risk. Mezei came to the United States in 1923 and lived for 25 years in Buffalo, N.Y., as a law-abiding person. He went to Rumania in 1948 to visit his aged mother. Conditions in Europe delayed his return until 1950. He returned with a visa in his pos-

There is only one instance in which a person seeking admission may have a measure of substantial protection; namely, when he claims to be a citizen of the United States. The act of 1952 provides[145] that if a person who is not within

---

session, issued by an American consul in Europe. At Ellis Island he was declared inadmissable on security grounds. The Government refused to tell him or the courts what information it had in its possession implicating him. He was twice shipped to Europe but neither France nor Great Britain accepted him. He applied to about a dozen countries in vain. Then he started *habeas corpus* proceedings, asserting that his detention for three years without a trial or even charges was illegal. The lower federal courts decided in his favor and ordered him released on bail, but the Supreme Court, by a five to four vote, reversed the decision. The court held that an alien seeking admission has no constitutional right to due process; he has no right to insist on being told the charges against him nor to be heard on the charges. A statute that permits the Attorney General to order an alien seeking admission or re-admission excluded without a hearing and without disclosing the information against him is constitutional. The courts will not review the decision of the Attorney General or compel him to disclose the charges or information.

Justices Black, Douglas, Frankfurter, and Jackson dissented. In his dissenting opinion Justice Douglas said:

> For nearly two years he was held in custody of the immigration authorities of the United States at Ellis Island, and if the Government has its way he seems likely to be detained indefinitely, perhaps for life, for a cause known only to the Attorney General.
>
> Our law, may and rightly does, place more restrictions on the alien than on the citizen. But basic fairness in hearing procedures does not vary with the status of the accused. If the procedures used to judge this alien are fair and just, no good reason can be given why they should not be extended to simplify the condemnation of citizens. If they would be unfair to citizens, we cannot defend the fairness of them when applied to the more helpless and handicapped alien.
>
> Quite unconsciously, I am sure, the Government's theory of custody for "safekeeping" without disclosure to the victim of charges, evidence, informers or reasons, even in an administrative proceeding, has unmistakenable overtones of the "protective custody" of the Nazis more than of any detaining procedure known to the common law.
>
> When indefinite confinement becomes the means of enforcing exclusion, it seems to me that due process requires that the alien be informed of its grounds and have a fair chance to overcome them. This is the more due him when he is entrapped into leaving the other shore by reliance on a visa which the Attorney General refuses to honor.

This case should be compared with Chew v. Colding, 73 S. Ct. 472 (1953), discussed in Chapter II, note 109.

[145] Sec. 360 (b) and (c).

the United States claims a right or privilege as a national[146] of the United States and is denied such right or privilege, he may make application to a diplomatic or consular officer for a certificate of identity for the purpose of traveling to the United States and applying for admission. If he is denied the certificate, he may appeal to the Secretary of State, who, if he approves the denial, shall state in writing the reasons for his decision. If the certificate is issued, the person then comes to a port of entry, and there he is subject to all provisions of the act relating to proceedings involving aliens. A final determination by the Attorney General that the person is not entitled to admission "shall be subject to review" in a *habeas corpus* proceeding.

How thorough the court's review would be remains to be seen. The courts may decide that it is ultimately a question for them as to whether the person seeking admission is *in fact* an alien or a citizen. In a case decided early in the twentieth century[147] two Justices of the Supreme Court,[148] in a dissenting opinion, challenged

> a system and provisions which place within the arbitrary power of an individual the denial of the right of an American citizen to free entrance into this country, and put such denial outside the scope of judicial inquiry. It may be true that a ministerial officer, in a secret and private investigation, may strive to ascertain the truth and to do justice, but unless we blind our eyes to the history of the long struggle in the mother country to secure protection to the liberty of the citizen, we must realize that a public investigation before a judicial tribunal, with the assistance of counsel, and the privilege of cross examination, is the best, if not the only, way to secure that result.[149]

[146] A "national" of the United States is one who is a citizen or who, though not a citizen, owes permanent allegiance to the United States. Sec. 101 (a) (21).

[147] U.S. v. Sing Tuck, 194 U.S. 161 (1904).

[148] Justices Brewer and Peckham, with opinion by the former.

[149] Cf. U.S. v. Ju Toy, 198 U.S. 253 (1905), in which Justice Brewer

Our discussion of the constitutional issues relating to both the substantive and the procedural aspects of our immigration policy leads to the conclusion that we must look to Congress, rather than to the courts, for the remedy of whatever defects we may find in the law. Americans must become reconciled to the fact that many phases of our immigration policy which ought to offend "a free-spirited society[150] are quite constitutional. The remedy for the defects must be sought in the "convictions and habits and actions,"[151] and in legislation that will reflect the wisdom and ideals, of the American community.

QUESTION OF WISDOM AND IDEALS

The Matter of Assimilation

In defending the act of 1952 which he sponsored, Senator McCarran[152] has said that, in his judgment, "assimilation is the key to a sound immigration system."[153] The national origins quota system, he has said,

> is not based on the premise of the superiority of Anglo-Saxon races but is based on the sound proposition that a preponderance of the population of the United States, its culture and institutions

also wrote a dissenting opinion, in which he was joined by Justices Peckham and Day. See also Quon Quon Poy v. Johnson, 273 U.S. 352 (1927); Chu Leung v. Shaughnessy, 83 F. Supp. 925 (1949).

[150] Justice Frankfurter, dis. op., West Virginia State Board of Education v. Barnette, 319 U.S. 624 (1943), at 670-671.

[151] *Ibid.*

[152] The members of Congress who originally voted for the McCarran-Walter measure, and then again voted for it in overriding President Truman's veto, are almost as much responsible for the act as are Senator Pat McCarran and Representative Francis E. Walter. Nothing said here or anywhere else in the book should be read as an attack on any one person or, for that matter, on any institution or agency of government. Our interest is exclusively in the merits of legislation, court decision, or other *official* conduct.

[153] Letter of Senator McCarran in *Christian Science Monitor,* January 10, 1953.

as a matter of historic fact stems from Northern and Western Europe and, therefore, the preponderance of immigration from Europe should be from Northern and Western Europe.[154]

The Senate committee of which Senator McCarran was chairman defended the national origins formula as a "rational and logical" method of numerically restricting immigration in such a manner that there would be preserved the "sociological and cultural balance" in the population of the United States. The peoples of western and northern Europe, said the committee, have made "the greatest contribution to the development of this country," and the committee was "fully justified" in restricting and directing immigration so that there would be admitted immigrants who could be considered "more readily assimilable" because of the similarity of their "cultural background" to those of the "principal components" of our population.[155]

In so far as expressed opinions are concerned, it would appear that this view represents only a small minority of Americans. At the hearings conducted by President Truman's Commission on Immigration and Naturalization, the statements of 634 persons and organizations were heard, but only a few raised their voices in defense of the national origins formula. (It may be assumed, however, that a large proportion of the 278 members of the House of Representatives and the 57 senators who voted to override President Truman's veto[156] were practical men who enjoyed some understanding of the views of their constituents, even if those views were and have continued to be largely unexpressed.) Only occasionally does one hear a defense of the national origins formula outside of Congress; an editorial in one of

[154] Quoted in article by Clayton Knowles in *New York Times* January 11, 1953.

[155] *Op. cit. supra* note 28, p. 455.

[156] *New York Times,* June 26 and 27, 1952.

America's leading newspapers has said that it is a "mistake" to condemn the formula as illiberal or as an expression of religious prejudice. It is, wrote the editor,

> no reflection on the many fine American citizens of all races, creeds and national origins to recognize realistically that some nations are far closer to the United States than others in culture, standard of living, respect for law, experience in self-government. Representatives of those nations, as a general rule, may be assimilated into American life more easily than others without causing the country "cultural indigestion." . . . we cannot agree that the basic system of national origin quotas is of itself an evil thing.[157]

There is nothing wrong, concluded the editor, with an immigration policy that attempts to balance humanitarian considerations against the "problems of cultural assimiliation in a 20th-century society."

The most respected defender of the national origins formula has been Professor Henry Pratt Fairchild.[158] It will be helpful if at this point we give a brief summary of his views as they have been expressed in his most recent work on the subject.[159]

Fairchild sees himself as a proponent of American nationality. The essence of nationality is, he says, a feeling—it is a feeling of identity as fellow members of a "we-group." Members of a nationality have the same or very similar "ideas, ideals, standards, aspirations, and life objectives." They are united

157 *Christian Science Monitor,* January 7, 1953. The editorial, while defending the national origins formula, criticises the act of 1952 for its many "unfair provisions," a phrase which the editorial quotes from a campaign speech by General Eisenhower.

158 H. P. Fairchild, *Immigration, a World Movement and Its American Significance* (1913, rev. ed. 1925); *The Melting-Pot Mistake* (1926).

159 *Race and Nationality as Factors in American Life* (1947). All quotations that follow in the text from Fairchild are from this book. Italics are added. Some of my observations with regard to Fairchild's views were previously stated in the *Saturday Review of Literature,* February 28, 1948.

in emotion and spirit, and they desire to share a common life. "They wish to be combined," he says, "in the ordering of their own essential institutions and enterprises. They wish to cooperate in the pursuit of their shared objectives. . . . They recognize a spiritual, emotional, and intellectual kinship, and on the basis of those bonds they wish to be united into a sympathetic, harmonious, and homogeneous unit." A lack of identity in language, religion, family system, economic structure, or the basic moral code is "a serious threat to nationality, and a detraction from its completeness." In the ideal nation the people speak a common language, have one religion and one body of moral traditions, and are descended from common ancestors. At the end of the American Revolution, the American people emerged, he says, "as a genuine nationality in its own right. All its essential characteristics were well established. *Later comers must logically be thought of as being admitted into a going nationality, not as helping to build one.*"

Into this American nationality, Professor Fairchild finds it difficult to fit many people, especially Jews and Negroes, the latter because of their race and color, the former because of their own nationality or cultural traits. The presence of these peoples operates prejudicially against genuine nationality. The laws which exclude certain racial groups from coming as immigrants and the national origins quota laws are justified as measures protecting our national integrity, or, rather, the degree of national integrity already achieved by us. We have gone as far as we could safely go in permitting, "in the name of humanitarianism and liberalism," the dilution of our nationality.

On St. Patrick's Day in 1945, Fairchild tells us, fifty thousand persons, linked to Ireland, marched up Fifth Avenue in the City of New York for almost four hours. This, he says, was only a single case, symbolic of many other processions that might take place, or have actually taken place, composed of Ukrainians, Lithuanians, Italians, Germans, Poles, and so on almost indefinitely. It is a mark of the essential liberalism of the United States that such a thing can occur. But it also raises the crucial question how far a nation can go in encouraging the persistence of groups, running into the second or even third generation, whose "hearts are linked inexorably" to some foreign land. A strong nationality can stand a good deal of this, but no nation can stand unlimited amounts of it.

America as a host, however, should always be courteous and just toward its guests. We must, says Fairchild, treat our aliens with consideration; we must try to root anti-Semitism out of our hearts; Jim Crow laws should be repealed; the Negro should be permitted to enjoy the franchise without special restrictions. "What liberals and progressives of every stamp should work for," he says, "is the humanizing of the heart of man."

Professor Fairchild's point of view is the angle from which the Senate Committee on the Judiciary and its Special Subcommittee to Investigate Immigration and Naturalization (both headed by Senator Pat McCarran) proceeded to conduct the general immigration investigation which culminated in a report of over 900 pages[160] and the McCarran-Walter Act. About a third of this report is devoted to statistics, which are intended to demonstrate the need to preserve the American nationality as projected by Fairchild. In 1790, we are reminded by the Senate committee report (as we have been reminded also by Fairchild), over 90 per cent of the white population was composed of English (83.5 per cent), Scotch (6.7 per cent), and Irish (1.6 per cent) stock. At that time there were "but six nationalities represented in the complexion of the Nation," while today "approxi-

[160] *Op. cit. supra* note 28.

mately 30 white nationality groups are component parts of our population."[161] The changes in nationality ratios are traced in painstaking fashion, with figures on the birth rates, criminality, mental affliction, education, relief, death rates, religion, sex, and other facts relating to the "races, peoples, and elements in the United States," beginning with Albanians from Europe and ending with Australians and New Zealanders. Each racial, religious, and national group is considered. The evaluation of the group's contribution to America is not made expressly; it is assumed, I suppose, that the facts will speak for themselves, and also that certain general observations will provide the reader with the framework within which he will himself be able to evaluate the groups and place them in his own mind in an order of merit.

Here are several of such general observations: "It is the distinctive fact regarding colonial immigration that it was Teutonic in blood and Protestant in religion."[162] The national origins system represents "the will of Congress to preserve the racial composition of the United States through the selection of immigrants from those countries whose traditions, languages, and political systems were akin to those of this country."[163] "Whereas the 'old immigration' [to 1880] was predominantly Teutonic in race and Protestant in religious belief, the 'new immigration' [1880-1925] was chiefly Latin, Slavic, and Semitic in race, and Catholic, Orthodox, and Jewish in religious belief."[164]

Here are several typical observations about specific groups in the United States. Of the Albanian—"Tribal and

[161] *Ibid.*, 80.
[162] *Ibid.*, 231, a quotation from J. R. Commons, *Races and Immigrants in America* (1907), 27.
[163] *Op. cit. supra* note 28, 442, a quotation from Helen F. Eckerson, "Immigrants and National Origins," *Monthly Review of the Immigration and Naturalization Service*, October 1945, p. 213.
[164] *Op. cit. supra* note 28, p. 235.

communal loyalty, the codes of ancient customs, and national pride are the dominant forces in his life."[165] The church has played a leading role among the Rumanian people, both gentiles and Jews. "Approximately 70 per cent of the people of Rumania are Greek Orthodox. . . . Approximately a third of the immigrants from Rumania were, however, Jews."[166]

Throughout the Senate committee report and underlying the national origins formula is the assumption that the immigrant must be "assimilated" "in the sense of being absorbed into the population through the loss of his peculiarities; he must successfully undergo a process of 'Americanization' whereby he was made to approximate an ideal American type."[167] We are brought back, at every turn in our study, to Senator McCarran's statement that "assimilation is the key to a sound immigration system."

There are many ways of answering Professor Fairchild and Senator McCarran. One answer is that "it takes two to assimilate."[168] Attitudes of prejudice and discriminating acts, which make the victims feel rejected and unwanted, lead to walls of separation between groups. It is adding insult to injury when those who, by their prejudices and discriminations, laid the foundation for these walls of separation climb to the top and, looking into the other camp, shout that the "out-group" resists assimilation.

> Distrustful of the apparent mental nonconformity of the immigrant, Americans took steps which made his assimilation more difficult. Feeling ourselves to be an in-group and the newcomers an out-group, we have segregated them in Little Italys and in

[165] *Ibid.*, 238. [166] *Ibid.*

[167] Stow Persons, "The Americanization of the Immigrant," in *Foreign Influences in American Life* (David F. Bowers, editor; 1944), 42.

[168] Senator G. F. Hoar, quoted in M. R. Coolidge, *Chinese Immigration* (1909), 423.

sections across the railroad tracks. Certain native Americans have tried to keep them from voting. We have excluded them from various organizations and institutions. And by these very acts of self-defense on our part we have delayed their adoption of our cherished values.[169]

But there is an answer which is more intimately a part of the American creed. This answer takes *freedom* and *individuality* as better keys than *assimilation* with which to unlock the treasures of the American genius, character, and culture.[170]

The Constitution, Mr. Justice Jackson has said, protects *the freedom to be intellectually and spiritually diverse or even contrary.* This freedom is enjoyed without fear that it will disintegrate the social organization. "We can have," he said,

> intellectual individualism and the rich cultural diversities that we owe to exceptional minds only at the price of occasional eccentricity and abnormal attitudes. When they are so harmless to others or to the State . . . , the price is not too great. But freedom to differ is not limited to things that do not matter much. That would be a mere shadow of freedom. The test of its substance is the right to differ as to things that touch the heart of the existing order. If there is any fixed star in our constitutional constellation, it is that no official, high or petty, can prescribe what shall be orthodox in politics, nationalism, religion, or other matters of opinion or force citizens to confess by word or act their faith therein.[171]

Where there is no "orthodoxy," there is no problem of

[169] J. G. Leyburn, "The Problem of Ethnic and National Impact from a Sociological Point of View," in *op. cit. supra* note 167, p. 61. Regarding the right to vote: now every state requires citizenship as a prerequisite, but this was not always the case. See Konvitz, *op. cit. supra* note 1, p. 1, footnote 2. Cf. *Yearbook on Human Rights for 1948* (U.N., 1950), table on p. 403.

[170] Myrdal, *An American Dilemma* (1944), Vol. I, ch. I.

[171] West Virginia State Board of Education v. Barnette, 319 U.S. 671 (1943), opinion for the court.

"assimilation." From the point of view expressed by the Supreme Court through Mr. Justice Jackson in the above passage, it is thoroughly "un-American" for Congress to adopt the "Teutonic-Protestant" strain in American culture as the essense of orthodox Americanism, and by this standard to find groups, derived from other "stocks" and identified with other religious strains, wanting in the essential ingredients of Americanism.

To use the concept of assimilation as the test of the quality of American society, and to conclude that large sections of the American people have failed by this test, is to say that America is to be judged by the touchstone that is relevant to countries like Spain or Greece or Libya, and that in comparison with their homogeneous societies American society is found defective. To approach American culture in this way is to look at it with the eyes of a foreigner. There is nothing more un-American than the attempt to mold America in conformance with the nationality concept that is at the bottom of our national origins formula. This has been well said by Mr. Justice Murphy:

> Distinctions based on color and ancestry are utterly inconsistent with our traditions and ideals. They are at variance with the principles for which we are now [1943] waging war. . . . To say that any group cannot be assimilated is to admit that the great American experiment has failed, that our way of life has failed when confronted with the normal attachment of certain groups to the lands of their forefathers.[172]

Forswearing past political allegiance and the assumption of American citizenship, Mr. Justice Frankfurter has said, are not at all inconsistent with cultural feeling imbedded in childhood and youth. A person may be a loyal American citizen, and fully at home here, and yet have an affinity with

[172] Conc. op. in Hirabayashi v. U.S., 320 U.S. 81 (1943).

other peoples and civilizations.[173] *Homo sum; humani nihil a me alienum puto.*[174] It is only in a totalitarian, closed society that an attempt is made to silence the "still, sad music of humanity" by making cultural nonconformance a criminal offense called "cosmopolitanism" or "idealism." It is only in a despotic society that the Catholic's concern with the Vatican or the Jew's concern with Jerusalem is punished as a heresy. We have found from our experience that we have fewer "enemy aliens" than have other nations, especially those that have built high walls of orthodoxy around them; for as the high walls have gone up, at the same time an underground has been started. In the course of World War II—in which Japan, Germany, and Italy were our chief enemies, and when we had within the United States 80,000 native-born and 47,000 foreign-born Japanese,[175] 1,623,000 foreign-born Italians, and 1,238,000 foreign-born Germans[176] —it was true that the United States, in its experience with millions of immigrants, had a contribution to make to the distraught world:

> We have, whether by sheer luck or by good common sense, effected a peaceful mingling of diverse cultures under freedom. . . . And now, in this present crisis [1944], we are being repaid with the loyalty of our so-called "enemy aliens" and of those of foreign stock. It is conceivable that our American experience might be taken as a model for post-war Europe.[177]

But Professor Fairchild and those who think like him want to fashion America after foreign models. It is an affront to their sense of Americanism to see fifty thousand persons, in

[173] Baumgarten v. U.S., 322 U.S. 665 (1944).
[174] Terence, *Heautontimoroumenos.*
[175] *Op. cit. supra* note 28, p. 144.
[176] *Ibid.,* 81.
[177] J. G. Leyburn, *op. cit. supra* note 169, p. 66. Immigrants admitted from 1820 to 1952 totalled 39,531,199. *The World Almanac* (1953), table on p. 643.

whose hearts Ireland occupies a special place, march up Fifth Avenue on St. Patrick's Day. Their patriotism is offended by the beards, the foot-washing, and the austerely plain dress of the Mennonites in Pennsylvania. Such feelings have no place in the hearts of Americans nor of human beings anywhere. Certainly they contradict the ideals of the America we know.

The Report of the President's Committee on Civil Rights (of which Charles E. Wilson was chairman) stated that the central theme in the American heritage is the individual person, and that the welfare of the individual is the final goal of the community. America knows no aristocracy, except " an aristocracy of talent and achievement." Our concept of equality, said the committee,

knows no kinship with notions of human uniformity or regimentation. We abhor the totalitarian arrogance which makes one man say that he will respect another man as his equal only if he has "*my* race, *my* religion, *my* political views, *my* social position." In our land men are equal, but they are free to be different. From these very differences among our people has come the great human and national strength of America.[178]

"In our land men are . . . *free to be different.*" These words echo the language of Jefferson, Madison, Emerson, Lincoln, Whitman, and William James. In our own day Horace Kallen has summed up this view of equality and freedom in his philosophy of cultural pluralism, of which the touchstone is the belief that men have the right—in a free, open society—to be intellectually, spiritually, culturally different; and not only different, but contrary, even cussedly contrary. Freedom stops only at the point where one creates a "clear and present danger" to an important social interest that the government may protect; or at the point where, as

[178] *To Secure These Rights* (1947), 4.

Sidney Hook has said, heresy is converted into conspiracy.[179] From this angle of vision, it is Fairchild, and not the "Irishman" who marched in the St. Patrick's Day parade, who is the stranger to American ways of thought and feeling.

Whatever may be true of other nations, ours is founded on the principle of *equality without uniformity.* Not cultural, religious, intellectual, or spiritual unity, but pluralism, is the bedrock on which is constructed American democracy. The Senate Committee on the Judiciary and its Special Subcommittee to Investigate Immigration and Naturalization may have spent several years preparing its 900-page report,[180] but it could not say that the lack of identities in religion, language, race, or what-not, has, *as a matter of established fact,* been found to constitute a threat to our nationality.

The colonists who came over here before the Revolution, says Professor Fairchild, were pioneers; they were men of great courage. The immigrants who followed them, however, the forefathers of more than half of the American people, were, on the contrary, "the unsuccessful, the weak, the dependent, the followers. . . ." It has been these weak, dependent, unsuccessful men and women and their children who, with their sweat and blood, with their very lives, have contributed to the building of the America that Fairchild and McCarran and all of us enjoy; who fought against their former homelands in order to secure, protect, and strengthen American nationality, which Congress misunderstands as long as it tolerates the notion, underlying the national origins formula, that Americans with English names are better

[179] Sidney Hook, *Heresy, Yes—Conspiracy, No* (1953).

[180] The Senate resolution (Res. 137) to investigate the immigration system was adopted July 26, 1947. The powers of the committee ended March 1, 1950. The authorized expenditure was $235,000. See Report, *op. cit. supra* note 28, p. 1.

people and better citizens than Americans with Italian, Greek, or Polish names.[181]

Were it not for our diversities, we would not be as free as we are. Were it not for our freedom, we would not be as strong as we are.

What can they know who only America know? How can they love America who only America love?[182]

Exclusion of Subversives

It would be difficult, if at all possible, for a loyal American to object to a law that would bar from entry as immigrants persons who are known to be members of the Communist party or connected with the party's apparatus. The conspiratorial character of the Communist party, and the aim of the party to subvert our democracy and to subject us, our minds, and our institutions to the will of the tyrants in the Kremlin, can no longer be doubted.[183] If the objective of the act of 1952 were limited to the exclusion from the United States of persons who, it is known, would be the tools of Soviet Russia, we could wholeheartedly approve the law.

But it is quite apparent from the provisions that the act may in part be used to carry on a war against what Senator Joseph R. McCarthy has called "Communist thinkers."[184] To

[181] Cf. President Truman's message vetoing the McCarran-Walter measure. Text in *New York Times*, June 26, 1952, and reprinted in the Appendix.

[182] Cf. Kipling: "What can they know who only England know?" For an answer to the pseudo-science of Fairchild, see *The Race Question in Modern Science*, a series of brochures by various authors, published by UNESCO, 1951-1952; Ashley Montague, *Statement on Race* (1951).

[183] Dennis v. U.S., 341 U.S. 494 (1951). Cf. Sidney Hook, "Does the Smith Act Threaten Our Liberties?" *Commentary* (January 1953), 63.

[184] In an interview, Senator McCarthy said that in the 83rd Congress he would conduct an investigation of American colleges and universities for the purpose of exposing "Communists and Communist thinkers—I'd rather use the words 'Communist thinkers' than 'Communists'" *U.S. News and World Report* (January 2, 1953), 31.

punish *thinkers* (Communist or anti-Communist) as distinguished from *actors* or *doers* (or co-conspirators) is to follow the Communist pattern. When Americans read that nearly a thousand Soviet economists and scientists gathered together in Moscow to admit publicly their errors in once praising the economic views of Nikolai A. Voznesensky, former Politburo member,[185] they think back to the book-burning days of the Nazis. There are, fortunately, no American precedents to which we can think back.[186] The government of the U.S.S.R. does not observe the "clear and present danger" test, according to which only individual actions and group conspiracies may be punished, while freedom of speech and the press remains inviolate and fully protected by the First Amendment to the Constitution. To a Communist, to think an unorthodox thought, to be an independent thinker, is to invite official persecution. While Russians look for non-Communist thinkers, are Americans going to look for Communist thinkers? If Americans will act in this fashion, there may ultimately be no difference between the kettle and the pot; both will be black.

To be a Communist thinker, one must be a *thinker,* an intellectual; e.g., a teacher. To be a teacher does not, of course, mean to be immune from laws that apply to all other persons. But a person in his capacity or vocation as a teacher enjoys the constitutional protection of freedom of speech and the press. This freedom is violated when the government seeks to punish him because he exercises his freedom in what some members of Congress would consider unorthodox ways. If the teacher becomes a member of the Communist conspiracy, he should be subject to the same penal-

[185] *New York Times,* January 9, 1953.

[186] We can recall the Tennessee evolution case of 1925, and some of the efforts to restrain freedom of teaching in American schools, discussed in H. K. Beale, *Are American Teachers Free?* (1936); but in the context of American history such incidents are aberrations rather than typical.

ties as those imposed upon lawyers, doctors, or union leaders who act in the same way. But to seek him out in his capacity as a *teacher* is to invade his basic freedoms.

This has been made clear by a unanimous United States Supreme Court in the Oklahoma case involving loyalty oaths.[187] A consideration of this case is quite relevant, as we shall see, to some of the provisions of the McCarran-Walter Act. It will help us to understand the distinction between the exclusion of known Communist doers or conspirators and the exclusion of persons suspected of being "Communist thinkers"; between thought control and the exclusion of totalitarians at Ellis Island.

In 1951 the Oklahoma legislature adopted an act that required all state officers and employees to take a prescribed oath. Several members of the faculty and staff of the Oklahoma Agricultural and Mechanical College failed to take the oath. A citizen-taxpayer brought a suit to enjoin state officials from paying them their salaries.

The persons who failed to take the oath objected chiefly to the following clauses:

> . . . That I am not affiliated directly or indirectly . . . with any foreign political agency, party, organization or government, or with any agency, party, organization, association, or group whatever which has been officially determined by the United States Attorney General or other authorized agency of the United States to be a communist front or subversive organization; . . . that I will take up arms in defense of the United States in time of war, or national emergency, if necessary; that within the five (5) years immediately preceding the taking of this oath (or affirmation) I have not been a member of . . . any agency, party, organization, association, or group whatever which has been officially determined by the United States Attorney General or

[187] Wieman v. Updegraff, 73 S. Ct. 215 (1952). See Konvitz, "Academic Freedom and Justice," *New Leader* (April 20, 1953).

other authorized public agency of the United States to be a communist front or subversive organization.

As the act was construed by the Oklahoma courts, the fact of membership alone disqualified a person from public employment. Previous decisions of the Supreme Court,[188] however, had upheld such oaths only if they disqualified a person on the basis of membership when he had knowledge concerning the organization to which he belonged; for membership may be innocent. A person, said Mr. Justice Clark for the court,

> may have joined a proscribed organization unaware of its activities and purposes. In recent years, many completely loyal persons have severed organizational ties after learning for the first time of the character of groups to which they had belonged. "They had joined, [but] did not know what it was; they were good, fine young men and women, loyal Americans, but they had been trapped into it—because one of the great weaknesses of all Americans, whether adult or youth, is to join something."[189] At the time of affiliation, a group itself may be innocent, only later coming under the influence of those who would turn it toward illegitimate ends. Conversely, an organization, formerly subversive and therefore designated as such may have subsequently freed itself from the influences which originally led to its listing.

The court held that the Oklahoma act offended the Due Process Clause of the Fourteenth Amendment by classifying indiscriminately *innocent* and *knowing* activity.

In his concurring opinion Mr. Justice Black contended that an American government does not have the power to punish "thought and speech as distinguished from acts." Our free society, he said,

[188] Garner v. Board of Public Works, 341 U.S. 716 (1915), involving a Los Angeles ordinance; Adler v. Board of Education, 342 U.S. 485 (1952), involving the Feinberg Law of New York; Gerende v. Board of Supervisors, 341 U.S. 56 (1951), involving a Maryland statute.

[189] Quotation from J. Edgar Hoover.

should never forget that laws which stigmatize and penalize thought and speech of the unorthodox have a way of reaching, ensnaring and silencing many more people than at first intended. We must have freedom of speech for all or we will in the long run have it for none but the cringing and the craven. And I cannot too often repeat my belief that the right to speak on matters of public concern must be wholly free or eventually be wholly lost.

It is self-evident that speech which criticises government and challenges current beliefs may be dangerous to the *status quo,* but, said Black, it was with full knowledge of this danger that the framers of the Constitution rested the First Amendment on the premise

that the slightest suppression of thought, speech, press, or public assembly is still more dangerous. This means that individuals are guaranteed an undiluted and unequivocal right to express themselves on questions of current public interest. It means that Americans discuss such questions as of right and not on sufferance of legislatures, courts or any other governmental agencies. It means that courts are without power to appraise and penalize utterances upon their notion that these utterances are dangerous.[190]

Mr. Justice Frankfurter, in a concurring opinion, emphasized the chief point in the decision of the court; namely, that the Oklahoma statute violated the freedom of association of the affected teachers because it required forswearing affiliation "which may well have been for reasons or for purposes as innocent as membership in a club of one of the established political parties." Freedom of speech, freedom of inquiry, and freedom of association are guaranteed to all persons, but the nature of the teacher's calling brings the constitutional safeguard "vividly into operation." Oklahoma's unwarranted inhibition upon the "free spirit of

[190] Justice Douglas concurred in this opinion.

teachers" has "an unmistakable tendency to chill that free play of the spirit which all teachers ought especially to cultivate and practice; it makes for caution and timidity in their associations by potential teachers." American democracy ultimately rests on public opinion; but to be our ultimate reliance, public opinion can be disciplined and responsible "only if habits of open-mindedness and of critical inquiry are acquired in the formative years of our citizens"; it becomes the special task of teachers to foster these habits of open-mindedness and critical inquiry. Teachers, as "the priests of our democracy," must be examples of open-mindedness and free inquiry. They cannot, however,

> carry out their noble task if the conditions for the practice of a responsible and critical mind are denied to them. They must have the freedom of responsible inquiry, by thought and action, into the meaning of social and economic ideas, into the checkered history of social and economic dogma. They must be free to sift evanescent doctrine, qualified by time and circumstance, from that restless, enduring process of extending the bounds of understanding and wisdom, to assure which the freedoms of thought, of speech, of inquiry, of worship are guaranteed by the Constitution of the United States against infraction by national or state government. The functions of educational institutions in our national life and the conditions under which alone they can adequately perform them are at the basis of these limitations upon state and national power.[191]

The decision of the court and opinions of Justices Clark, Black, and Frankfurter are consistent with the court's decision in the *Dennis* case.[192] Taking the cases together, it seems that the Supreme Court has held that the federal or a state government may, without thereby infringing the First Amendment, punish membership in a group when (1)

[191] Justice Douglas concurred in this opinion also.
[192] Dennis v. U.S., cited *supra* note 183.

the group is formed for the purpose of teaching and advocating the overthrow of the government by force and violence, and (2) membership in the group is held voluntarily, with knowledge of its subversive activities and purposes.

If the member knows only of the organization's legitimate purposes—e.g., to engage in collective bargaining, if it is a trade union; to sell books at a discount, if it is a book club; to further the professional interests of lawyers and improve the administration of justice, if it is a lawyers' organization; to seek to elect to public office candidates who are pledged to a program of international peace, though its achievement may involve a large measure of appeasement, if it is a political party—his membership is innocent and is protected by the Constitution. The fact may well be that the organization may use its legitimate program only as a facade behind which the inner apparatus is free to carry on subversive activities, making the organization in fact a tool of the Communist Party and of the U.S.S.R.—the C.I.O. in 1949 found that eleven of its affiliated unions were operated in this way, and felt itself compelled to expel them as Communist-controlled unions, though it meant a loss of about 800,000 members.[193] But if the member sees only the front and is unaware of the behind-the-scenes trickery, or does not believe that the disclosures about the organization are true, then his membership is innocent and is protected by the Constitution.

"He ought to know better!" we are inclined to say. Certainly he ought to know better. But to punish him by loss of his employment or by sending him to prison because he does not know better is to punish him for the state of his mind. If, however, he is in the organization with full knowl-

[193] See *Communist Domination of Certain Unions* (1951), Report of Senate Subcommittee on Labor and Labor-Management Relations, Senate Document 89, 82d Cong., 1st sess. See also other reports of the subcommittee (Senator Hubert H. Humphrey, chairman) on this subject.

edge that it is in fact a Communist party tool, then if he is punished, the punishment is for his *action,* for being a member of a criminal conspiracy, for knowingly being a co-conspirator.

It seems paradoxical that the Constitution should protect thought from any form of government control, yet should make thought an indispensable ingredient of a criminal offense. The paradox is not real, however, for what the law may constitutionally punish is *action,* and not thought; but action without thought may be as innocent as the behavior of a very young child, or of a somnambulist, or of a lunatic. In order to protect "the freedoms of thought, of speech, of inquiry, of worship," guaranteed by the Constitution, the Supreme Court has been compelled to emphasize that membership in an organization may be made subject to punishment only if it is maintained *knowingly,* i.e., with full awareness that the organization is in fact a criminal conspiracy.[194]

It is, then, not enough to prove that a person is a "Communist thinker"; there must be proof that he is a Communist actor: the thinking must be absorbed in the action; the action must be that of a Communist thinker. Communist

[194] The courts have not yet been faced with the question of membership in, e.g., the International Fur and Leather Workers' Union, with a membership of about 100,000, by a person who knows that the union is Communist-dominated, though he himself is anti-Communist, but who must maintain his membership if he is to hold his job.

The Supreme Court will need to face one day the question involving a member of the Communist party who is not in the inner circle of leaders but is rather on the periphery of the organization because he is new and must still prove his loyalty to the party. He may have no personal knowledge of the subversive character of the party, nor believe what he has read or been told: that the party is a tool of the Kremlin. Does his case show that combination of action and thought which would subject him to legal penalties without violation of his constitutional freedoms? As the court's precendents stand at this time (early in 1953), it would seem that he could not be convicted under the Smith Act as a co-conspirator. This was Judge Edw. J. Dimock's position as he freed Simon W. Gerson and Isidore Begun in the trial of secondary Communist party leaders in New York in 1952-53. Cf. Deuteronomy 19:4-13.

thinking is, therefore, a necessary ingredient of the act which is the offense. Communist thinking alone is not enough. There must be Communist action by a Communist thinker. The offense, however, is in the action; this is the point that is explicated by Justices Black and Frankfurter in the concurring opinions with which the decisions of the court in the *Dennis* and the loyalty oath cases are consonant.

If we keep this analysis in mind as we study the McCarran-Walter Act, it becomes apparent that some of its provisions, by going beyond what the Constitution permits with respect to a denial of fundamental freedoms guaranteed to Americans, tend to contribute to an atmosphere which, Mr. Justice Black has said, makes "the present period of fear" seem "more ominously dangerous to speech and press than was that of the Alien and Sedition Laws." The Oklahoma oath statute, he said, "is but one mainfestation of a national network of laws aimed at coercing and controlling the minds of men."[195] The McCarran-Walter Act is another such manifestation. Even if it is a law that applies only to *foreigners,* it is part of the "network of laws" because it is an expression of *citizens.* We ban the entry of narcotic drug addicts; we also have special laws that prohibit traffic in narcotic drugs within the United States. We ban the entry of persons who offend us only by reason of their thoughts; we, who are responsible for the ban, must believe that dangerous thoughts are in some way subject to governmental control.

The publisher of the *New York Times* has asserted that Americans were not as free to speak their minds in 1953 as they were in 1933. "There has been dropped upon utterance and thought," he said,

> a smoke screen of intimidation that dims essential thought and essential talk and begets a fog through which we wander un-

[195] Case cited *supra* note 187.

certainly. Nor is it the super-zealots who bother me so much in all of this—it is the lack of plain, old-fashioned guts on the part of those who capitulate to them. Surely, such actions must be of great aid and comfort to the Kremlin; these capitulators are, in effect, a sixth column which does not even require payment.[196]

The McCarran-Walter Act is part of this smoke screen of intimidation that has been dropped upon utterance and thought. We shall cite a number of the ways in which this is done.

"Some months ago," the American Committee for Cultural Freedom[197] reported,

> the United States government asked the Norwegian labor movement to send a delegation of trade union leaders to this country. This delegation was to take the form of a Study Commission, which would examine at first hand the way of life of the American worker, and which would then report its findings to the Norwegian people. The Norwegian unions nominated nine of their outstanding personalities to the Study Commission. Imagine their consternation when the State Department then informed them that four of their nominees could not be granted visas until their life-histories had been subjected to a more intensive scrutiny!
>
> What was the reason for the State Department's action? One of the nominees, a venerable labor journalist and an outstanding anti-Communist, had been affiliated with the Norwegian Com-

[196] Arthur Hays Sulzberger in *New York Times,* January 15, 1953, upon receipt of the Alexander Hamilton Medal of the Association of the Alumni of Columbia College.

[197] This organization has in its leadership Sidney Hook, Arthur Schlesinger, Jr., and other outstanding intellectuals who have led the struggle against Communism for many years. The Congress for Cultural Freedom, an international organization with which the American Committee is affiliated, is led by, among others, Karl Jaspers, Salvador de Madariaga, Jacques Maritain, Reinhold Niebuhr, Bertrand Russell, Denis de Rougemont, Sidney Hook, Ignazio Silone, and Stephen Spender. "A Memorandum on the Visa Problem," published in the December, 1952, *Bulletin* of the American Committee, is reprinted in full in the Appendix. The quotations in the text are from this publication.

munist movement in the early 1920's. A second nominee had visited Russia at the request of the Norwegian labor movement —but had written so hostile a report that the United States Government had reprinted it and distributed it all over the world. The third nominee had been mistaken by the State Department for someone else. The case of the fourth nominee, who had never been connected with any Communist activities, was inexplicable and remains so to this day; presumably he was the victim of a false and malicious "confidential denunciation."

This was not a solitary case: "Unfortunately, there have been more than a few such incidents." Many such incidents, involving outstanding scientists, are reported in a special issue of the *Bulletin of the Atomic Scientists.*[198] Herbert Agar has described the sort of situation that has been created by the McCarran-Walter Act.[199] Let us, he says,

> picture a famous European man of science, or of letters, who has been invited to a conference in the United States by his American colleagues. He goes to our embassy in his own country to seek a visa. He is given forms to fill out which are an insult and an absurdity: an insult because they seem to presuppose that he is a potential enemy who has to prove his innocence; an absurdity because he is asked to testify on the spot, to exactly what he thought, or wrote, or believed, forty years ago.[200] He is then interviewed by a harassed consular official, again on the assumption that a distinguished foreigner (honored, requested, and awaited by his American confreres) is probably a fraud, and that he must somehow reassure us that he has not been lying. Finally, his papers go forward to Washington. There, in a land

[198] "American Visa Policy and Foreign Scientists," in the October 1952 issue of the *Bulletin.*

[199] It should be recalled that much of our trouble in this connection originated in the Internal Security Act of 1950, the relevant sections of which have been incorporated in the act of 1952.

[200] "Why should an applicant [for a visa] have to give the exact address and exact dates of every place of residence since the day he was born? How many State Department officials or Congressmen can answer such a question honestly and accurately?" *Op. cit. supra* note 197.

of abused and overworked bureaucrats, the dreary forms and timid reports are

> upwhirled aloft
> Fly o'er the backside of the world far off
> Into a limbo large and broad, since called
> The Paradise of Fools.

Emerging at last from this Miltonic chaos, the papers return to their point of origin. And the great man receives his visa several months after the conference to which he was invited has come to an end.[201]

Our present legal provisions and administrative procedures have a restricting and discrediting effect upon our fundamental freedoms (as well as harmful effects on our country's position in the family of democratic, free nations). With our discussion of the *Dennis* and loyalty-oath cases in mind, it is not difficult to indicate lines along which the McCarran-Walter Act should be amended.[202]

The law should prohibit the entry of aliens who are members of or affiliated with subversive organizations if membership or affiliation was maintained voluntarily and knowingly, i.e., for the purpose of supporting the subversive policies and the program. If the alien is admittedly a member of or affiliated with a subversive organization, the burden of proving that he does not voluntarily and knowingly support its subversive policies and program may rest on him.

If only *past* membership or affiliation is involved, there should be no need to prove "active" opposition to the organization for the past five years. It should be enough that the

[201] Herbert Agar, "A Prayer for the New President," *Saturday Review of Literature* (January 17, 1953), 8; quoted with permission of the publisher.

[202] Cf. the recommendations of the American Committee for Cultural Freedom, reprinted in the Appendix, and the recommendations in the report of the President's Commission on Immigration and Naturalization, *Whom We Shall Welcome,* ch. XV.

alien has cut himself free from the organization and is now, by conviction, opposed to its subversive character.

To be sure, it is conceivable that a Communist agent will give the appearance of having become nonpolitical, in order better to deceive. But it is no less conceivable that he will, if necessary, pose as an active anti-Communist. Communist subversion is too protean a force to be calculated and measured definitely by any law, and administrative intelligence will always be needed for the determination of any concrete case.[203]

As we saw in the case of Ellen Knauff, aliens may be excluded without a hearing, and on the basis of information of a confidential nature, which need not be disclosed. Until recently such exclusions were rare; but in the year and a half prior to July 1952, approximately two thousand aliens were excluded without a hearing.[204] The act of 1952 does not limit the power to exclude without a hearing to a time of war or national emergency. Such a power should not be exercised "except in the extreme and unusual case where the national security or the lives, welfare, or continual usefulness of our intelligence agents and informants are immediately affected by the fact that the very holding of a hearing will cause disclosure of highly secret information."[205] The determination as to whether the alien should be excluded without a hearing, on the basis of confidential infor-

[203] *Op. cit. supra* note 197. The report of the President's Commission on Immigration and Naturalization points out that the requirement of five years' active opposition to a totalitarian ideology may defeat important objectives of our intelligence and foreign policy agencies. There may be "conclusive proof" of complete reformation in a shorter period of time. The requirement of "active" opposition to totalitarian ideology also misses the point. "Most people who have genuinely renounced subversive ideas do not become active pamphleteers. . . ; the genuineness of their opposition to totalitarianism cannot be measured by the loudness of their disclaimers." *Op. cit. supra* note 202, p. 227.

[204] *Whom We Shall Welcome*, 229. [205] *Ibid.*, 230.

mation, should be made by a statutory Board of Immigration and Visa Appeals.[206]

The most important procedural change that can be made is one that is suggested by a phrase in Mr. Justice Frankfurter's dissenting opinion in the *Knauff* case. The privilege of entry is, said Frankfurter, one which Congress may grant or withhold; but in the case of war brides, he said, the privilege of entry was extended by Congress "for the benefit not of the alien but of her American husband. . . ."

This brief remark by Frankfurter opens up vistas of legal principles and procedures which heretofore have been only dimly seen. As matters stand now, in every situation involving an alien knocking on our door for admission, attention is focused only on the alien. He may seek entry because he has been invited by a son or a father, or other close relative, or by a distinguished university, or by a responsible church or synagogue, or by a committee of famous scholars who are planning an international conference. Such circumstances may, in some instances, put the alien in a preferred class substantively, but procedurally such facts will make little difference. The case never becomes one involving the rights of the American citizens who seek the alien's admission. The sponsoring citizens do not enjoy any special legal status or rights in the proceedings.

On the contrary, sponsors are often treated as unwelcome intruders; their appearance, even on the fringes of the proceedings, is often resented. I recall that some years ago I was called to Washington to testify before a board of inquiry with regard to the application for admission into the United States of a French scholar to whom I was related and whose application I sponsored. My examination was *in camera,* and I still recall with pain and humiliation the way I was treated. One might have thought that I had been

[206] *Ibid.,* 231.

caught smuggling into the country obscene and lewd picture post cards. There was not the slightest evidence of an awareness that the sponsor, an American citizen, had any legitimate interests, let alone rights, that deserved respect.[207]

Mr. Justice Frankfurter's point of view in the *Knauff* case received broad (and prior) expression in a statement presented in 1948 to the Immigration Subcommittee of the Senate Judiciary Committee on behalf of the American Jewish Committee and associated organizations.[208]

An American citizen, the statement submits, when he is willing to sponsor an immigrant (and to guarantee against his becoming a public charge),

> should be recognized as having sufficient interest in a visa application case to have standing to take an appeal. On such appeal the same standards that are fixed by the Administrative Procedure Act for appeals from other administrative decisions should be made applicable. In effect, this would mean that a consular decision could be set aside, on appeal, if the decision were based upon an error of law or if there were no "substantial evidence" to support the initial decision.[209]

What justification can there be for this radical change in our angle of vision in exclusion cases? The statement of the American Jewish Committee provides the answer:

[207] The alien in question was admitted—a fact which shows that there was nothing in *his* record that could account for the treatment of the sponsor; and the fact that the alien was admitted shows that the sponsor's record had also been cleared.

[208] The statement has been published as a pamphlet, *Americanizing Our Immigration Laws* (New York: American Jewish Committee, 1949). It was prepared by Felix S. Cohen, with the collaboration of Oscar Handlin, Mortimer Spiegelman, and Sidney Liskofsky.

[209] *Ibid.*, 75. The President's Commission does not go as far. See Commission report, *op. cit. supra* note 202, pp. 146-167. The Commission recommends the right of an appeal to the alien from the denial of a visa by the consular officer; apparently no such right for the sponsor is, however, contemplated; and the Commission does not believe that the Administrative Procedure Act should apply to the exclusion process. With regard to these matters, I believe the recommendations in the statement cited in note 208 *supra* are preferable.

An American citizen who imports Swiss cheese can invoke the Administrative Procedure Act and even go to a Court of Customs Appeals if he is dissatisfied with the decisions of the bureaus. But if he wants to import the Swiss cheese maker, and set up a new local industry here and employ native Americans in that industry, he is told that he must swallow whatever decision the bureaus make, without complaining. There is no sense in that. Certainly it is not in accord with the American idea of the proper relation between citizens and their public servants. . . . Why should not an American citizen interested in such a case have a right of appeal . . . such as we give to American citizens in almost every other field of our national life? Every step that our Congress can take to refocus our immigration procedures on the interests of American citizens will be a step towards the elimination of uneconomic and un-American bureaucracy. If we really want to Americanize our immigrants, we might begin by Americanizing our immigration laws.[210]

The most effective way to Americanize the procedure in our immigration laws is, as we have said, to recognize the legal status and rights of the American citizen, group of citizens, or institution that sponsors and seeks the alien's admission. Once it is acknowledged that a specific American has a legitimate interest in the proceedings, it should not be difficult to give such legal expression to that interest as would adequately demonstrate that the importation of human beings, like the importation of cheese or machinery or books, is subject to a government of laws, not of men. No element of security protection need be sacrificed, or even jeopardized, by this change in point of view.[211]

[210] *Op. cit, supra* note 208, p. 17.

[211] The President's Commission recommended the elimination of the national origins quota system and the substitution of a unified quota system, based on the 1950 census. There would be a quota of 251,162 aliens to be admitted annually, in accordance with the following five categories: (1) right of asylum, (2) reunion of families, (3) needs in the United States, (4) special needs in the free world, and (5) general immigration. *Op. cit. supra* note 202, pp. 118 ff. The interest of specific American citizens would

CONCLUSION

In his first State of the Union Message, President Eisenhower spoke of the discriminatory and unjust aspects of our quota system,[212] thus repeating and underscoring the attack on the McCarran-Walter Act which he made in his campaign speech at Newark, New Jersey.[213]

There are two rights, the President told Congress, that the government manifestly has in the field of immigration; namely, to limit the number of immigrants in conformance with the country's absorptive capacity, and to set reasonable requirements on the character of immigrants. These rights, however, must be asserted in such a way that our nation will remain "faithful to our basic ideas of freedom and fairness to all." It is well to remind ourselves occasionally, he said, that "we are—one and all—immigrants or the sons and daughters of immigrants." (This reminder, it is interesting to note, is found often in writings and speeches on the subject of American immigration policy as an echo of the Biblical refrain: "And thou shalt remember that thou wast a bondman [or slave] in the land of Egypt, and the Lord thy God redeemed thee; therefore I command thee this thing today."[214])

The McCarran-Walter Act, the President continued, contains "injustices." "It does, in fact, discriminate." He added that he had been informed by members of Congress that it was realized when the statute was enacted that "future

---

be easiest to establish in categories 1, 2, and 3. With regard to the other categories, the chief burden of establishing a basis for admission might rest on the alien himself. The Commission recommends, as we have noted, improved procedures to assure the alien a fair hearing and a review of consular decisions. *Ibid.*, ch. xi.

[212] Message of February 2, 1953. Text in *New York Times*, February 3, 1953. See appendix III.

[213] Text in *New York Times*, October 18, 1952.

[214] Deut. 24:18.

study of the proper basis of determining quotas would be necessary." He, therefore, called upon Congress to review the statute and to enact legislation "which will at one and the same time guard our legitimate national interest and be faithful to our basic ideas of freedom and fairness to all."

1. If Congress were to set for itself the goal of eliminating from the act all vestiges of discrimination, it would repeal the Asia-Pacific triangle provision. The repeal of this provision is not likely to serve as a signal for the influx of many thousands of persons of Oriental extraction from Latin America as nonquota immigrants.

As we have seen, Latin Americans, although free to enter the United States on a nonquota basis, have not come here in large numbers. "During the past 127 years [prior to 1949] only about 11,000 immigrants a year, on the average, have come from south of the border."[215] There is no reason to assume that Latin Americans of Oriental extraction are likely to behave differently from their neighbors and attempt to come to the United States as an overwhelming flood of humankind. The reasons that are relevant for their neighbors are equally relevant for them. What are some of the reasons that keep Latin Americans from taking advantage of the nonquota preferential treatment which our laws have offered them?

> The fact is that most people south of our borders . . . do not want to leave their homes in order to improve their condition or the opportunities for their children. . . Outside of this country, most people are rooted to the soil, unwilling to move to strange lands and learn strange ways. Most people, in foreign lands, grow up and die in the localities where they were born.[216]

In addition to the force of inertia, there are other factors

[215] *Op. cit. supra* note 208, pp. 8-9.
[216] *Ibid.*, 9.

that keep Latin Americans home: they do not have American citizens who would be willing to sponsor their entry and to guarantee that they would not become public charges, and they do not have the other qualifications our statute and regulations require.[217]

2. Congress would repeal, too, the provision which creates a subquota for immigrants born in colonial or dependent areas of the Western Hemisphere. This provision, as we have seen, gives Jamaicans (Negroes) a statutory quota of 100, while other persons from the Western Hemisphere (except those of Oriental extraction) may come here without quota limitations. Immigration from Jamaica has averaged 1,000 per year. Is it worth our while to make our immigration law racist in character because of these few Negro immigrants? Are we not repeating here the tragic mistake and injustice of our Chinese and Japanese exclusion laws? Have Americans learned nothing from that miserable experience?

3. Regarding the national origins quota formula, the recommendations of the President's Commission on Immigration and Naturalization seem to offer a wise solution to the problem. The Commission's recommendations may be summarized as follows: the complete abolition of the national origins system; an annual quota of approximately 250,000 immigrants;[218] within this maximum, visas should be issued in accordance with the following five categories:

(a) The right of asylum, available for refugees, escapees, expellees, and other persons suffering from political, religious, and economic persecution. A temporary priority should be given persons in this category by providing for an annual admission of 100,000 refugees and other dis-

[217] *Ibid.*, 9-10.

[218] The figure is 251,162, representing one-sixth of one per cent of the population of the United States as shown by the 1950 (instead of the 1920) census.

placed persons over a three-year period. This provision would help solve the existing emergency within the immigration pattern.

(b) Reunion of families; i.e., immigrants whose admission would result in reuniting families.

(c) Needs in the United States; i.e., persons with skills to fill needs as certified by appropriate officials.

(d) Special needs in the free world. In the interests of world peace and security, America should help relieve the overpopulation problem in countries of the free world.[219]

(e) General immigration of all other qualified persons, without allowing any one country or area unfair advantages over others.

The Commission recommends continuance of the nonquota status for persons born in the Western Hemisphere, but without regard to race or color and without discrimination against colonies.

Should Congress, however, not wish to repeal the national origins formula, then the least it could do is accept the pattern proposed by Senators Lehman and Humphrey and their colleagues in S. 2842, the bill offered as a substitute for the McCarran-Walter bill. It provided that an annual quota be allotted to each country, based on the national origins principle; but the census of 1950, instead of 1920, would be used as a basis for the computation. These

[219] The Intergovernmental Committee for European Migration, of which Hugh S. Gibson is director, estimated that western and central Europe's minimum migration requirement is about 5,000,000 persons. Italy, Greece, Western Germany, the Netherlands, and Austria are seriously over populated. Potential areas of resettlement are Brazil, Argentina, Colombia, Venezuela, Canada, Australia, and the United States. See report by Michael L. Hoffman in *New York Times,* January 13, 1953. Cf. L. Dudley Stamp, *Land for Tomorrow: The Underdeveloped World* (1952); Josue de Castro, *The Geography of Hunger* (1952).

quotas are not to be reduced by the admissions that took place under the displaced persons legislation. Visas would be allotted as follows: (1) the first 50 per cent of each area's quota would be available to qualified persons whose services are urgently needed in the United States, and their accompanying families; (2) the next 20 per cent to spouses or children of resident aliens; (3) the remaining 30 per cent to other qualified immigrants, with preferences given to brothers, sisters, sons, or daughters of citizens, and parents of resident aliens.

Perhaps the most significant provision in the bill with regard to quotas is that all unissued or unused quota numbers would be assigned to a general quota pool and be available, without reference to national origins, for the following purposes: (1) family reunion preferences, to a maximum of 25 per cent of the pooled quota numbers, to admit adult children, brothers and sisters, and other blood relatives of citizens, and spouses, minor and adult children, parents, brothers and sisters, and other blood relatives of resident aliens; (2) national need preferences, to a maximum of 25 per cent of the pooled quota numbers, to admit persons of special ability whose services are urgently needed in the United States, or who are likely to be of special benefit to the national economy, cultural interests, or welfare of the United States; (3) persecuted persons, to a maximum of 25 per cent of the pooled quota numbers; and (4) nonpreference cases: American citizens or institutions may apply to the Secretary of State for the admission of immigrants whose cases merit special consideration because of special hardship or circumstances.

The quota system proposed in S. 2842 is obviously a compromise: some immigrants would be admitted under the restrictions of a national origins formula and quota; some would be admitted without regard to national labels. Had this system been in effect in the years 1925-52, it would have worked in the following way:

Total quota numbers available	4,362,354
Total quota numbers allotted for use	1,923,509
Total admitted under pooled quota	2,438,845

In other words, about two million (or 44 per cent of the total) immigrants would have come in under national origins quotas; about two and a half million (or 56 per cent) would have come in without regard to national origins or national quotas. (Under the quota laws of Congress, the two and a half million persons were *not* admitted; the quota numbers were just not used.)

Since, under existing law, so large a proportion of quota numbers are unused because quotas from some countries in northern and western Europe are undersubscribed, the pooled quotas would be used mainly by immigrants from southern and eastern Europe and from other parts of the world. This means that under S. 2842, countries of southern and eastern Europe and of other parts of the world (except the Western Hemisphere) would in effect have national quotas, as heretofore, and limited nonquota status. The pooled quotas would benefit the peoples who are now suffering from national origins discrimination.

This issue Congress cannot evade. If it is going to enlarge substantially the quota numbers available for the peoples currently discriminated against by providing them with a quota pool, it might as well act openly, candidly, and graciously by abolishing the national origins formula altogether. To adopt any compromise would be to maintain a discriminatory principle in shadow, while having a nondiscriminatory immigration policy in substance. In the field of civil liberties, shadow and substance should conform; for often people will judge that what is apparent exists, and will judge only by appearances.

4. Professors should be restored to nonquota immigrant status. In the years 1925-1948 we admitted as nonquota immigrants a total of 2,869 professors of institutions of higher learning.[220] Similar status was enjoyed by ministers of religious denominations, of whom 8,364 were admitted in the same years.[221] The 1952 act retained the provision regarding ministers but dropped that relating to professors. No reason has been offered for this action by Congress.[222] It has been suggested that the action is another indication of "the suspicious uneasiness concerning the reliability of the highly educated."[223] While there is an American belief that everyone has a right to higher education,[224] "those who devote their lives to science and scholarship are distrusted."[225] Patronizing distrust has been changed into "active and harassing suspicion."[226] The undertaking to look for "Communist thinkers" on American campuses is an indication of the same phenomenon.

One is reminded in this connection of what happened to Miguel de Unamuno. At the beginning of the academic term in 1936 Unamuno, as Rector of the University at Salamanca, rose to speak in Ceremonial Hall. Preceding him, there had spoken a general of Franco's army, who abused the "bad Spaniards" on the Republican side. When Unamuno declared that there were good and bad Spaniards on each side, he was shouted down, and someone cried: "Death to the intelligentsia!"[227]

[220] *Op. cit. supra* note 28, table on p. 821. [221] *Ibid.*

[222] See *Ibid.*, 474-476. [223] *Op. cit. supra* note 95, p. 213.

[224] *Higher Education for American Democracy*, Report of President's Commission on Higher Education (1947).

[225] *Op. cit. supra* note 95, p. 213. [226] *Ibid.*

[227] Arturo Barea, *Unamuno* (1952), 57. The author, translating the cry *Muera la inteligencia!* says perhaps it should be translated as "Death to the Intelligence!"

The exemption from quota status of professors is not as significant as is the repeal of the exemption once it has been granted. To withdraw the exemption after its existence in our laws for over a quarter of a century is to give the action of Congress a symbolic meaning that can do American culture no good; for it can be, and has been, taken to mean as an international affront to scholars and scientists—to scholarship and science—to the intelligence.

5. These observations lead naturally to a consideration of other provisions in the act of 1952 which fall with a special impact on scholars and scientists; viz., the provisions relating to subversives, which reflect a commendable concern to keep Communists off our shores, yet serve as

> only one more illustration of this contradictory belief in the supreme importance of scientific knowledge and the terrible fear of scientists as the unreliable, untrustworthy vessels of this knowledge.
>
> The excessive preoccupation with the dangers of revolutionary subversion, arising from a compound of xenophobia, distrust of intellectual activity, and the animosity of the professional politician against the usually better educated civil servants . . . brings us to our present position.[228]

There can be no question of the proposition that "legislation which establishes an absolute bar against admission to the United States of those whose purpose in entering is to engage in activities which violate our laws relating to espionage, sabotage, public disorder or national security must remain on our statute books and be strictly enforced."[229]

Nor can there be any doubt that persons who are currently members of or affiliated with subversive organizations should be barred from entry if they intended by member-

[228] *Op. cit. supra* note 95, pp. 213-214

[229] *Whom We Shall Welcome*, p. 221.

ship or affiliation to further the subversive purposes of the organization.

A financial contribution or pledge to an organization should not, standing alone, create a presumption of affiliation, unless the act was done with the intention to further the subversive aims and principles of the organization.[230] A union member in Italy or France may be compelled, in order to hold his job, to make a contribution to an organization that we would consider subversive, though at heart he may wish the group nothing short of its utter ruin and destruction.

The act should prohibit the admission of members of all totalitarian organizations—Nazi and Fascist, as well as Communist. Some persons would require from immigrants a pledge to support freedom and democracy in the United States, and the American Constitution. I see no need for this; we should afford them an opportunity to find out for themselves what American institutions and ideals signify, so that the terms and concepts will be meaningful to them rather than merely elements in a compulsory ceremony. But persons who are "hostile to our way of life" and adherents of totalitarianism should be barred.[231]

Past membership in or affiliation with a subversive organization should not bar entry, if such membership or affiliation was involuntary, without regard to the age of the person when he was a member or an affiliate; without regard to the fact that he severed his relation with the organization five years or one year ago; and without regard to the question whether he has been, since termination of membership or affiliation, "actively opposed" to subversive ideologies. It is rare, "that a record of a person's political biography speaks unambiguously for itself; more generally, the significance to

[230] *Ibid.*, 222-223. [231] *Ibid.*, 225.

be attached to any parts of this record, or to the whole of it, has to be supplied by the informed and intelligent observer—in this case, the consul in charge of issuing visas."[232] External indicia may camouflage the guilty or penalize the innocent. They ought to have evidentiary value but be subject to intelligent and informed interpretation by responsible officials, who should be guided in part by the belief that "the removal of the absolute bar against former—and now reformed—subversive aliens strengthens our own internal and external security and advances our foreign policy."[233]

6. Procedurally, the most important change that can be introduced in immigration policy is to give statutory recognition to the interests of the American citizen or resident alien who sponsors the admission of the immigrant. This recognition would provide a foundation for a configuration of rights of which the sponsor and the alien would be the beneficiaries. It would have the effect of reducing to a minimum the chances of arbitrary official conduct and discriminatory action. It would provide the alien with an advocate who does have constitutional rights and guarantees.[234]

If this change were effected in our immigration policy, it would become apparent that immigration procedure should be made to conform with the Administrative Procedure Act; for "American citizens who are interested in immigration cases should have just as much protection as the Administrative Procedure Act affords to any other citizen interested in the processes of government."[235]

The act of 1952, it will be recalled, authorizes the exclusion of aliens without any hearing in security cases.[236] The

[232] *Op. cit. supra* note 197. [233] *Op. cit. supra* note 229, 227.

[234] See note 211 *supra*.

[235] *Op. cit. supra* note 208, p. 17. This recommendation goes beyond that of the President's Commission, which recommended conformity with the Administrative Procedure Act only in deportation cases. See *op. cit. supra* note 229, ch. xi, especially pp. 158-160, 166, 170.

[236] Cf. Ellen Knauff case, in which such exclusion was based on a 1941

power to exclude without a hearing "should not be exercised except in the extreme and unusual case where the national security or the lives, welfare, or continued usefulness of our intelligence agents and informants are immediately affected by the fact that the very holding of a hearing will cause disclosure of highly secret information."[237]

The procedure with regard to the issuance of visas to scientists and scholars should be made to conform to the recommendations of the President's Commission[238] and those of the American Committee for Cultural Freedom.[239] Unless such persons are permitted access to their American colleagues, "American science loses the benefit of the potential contribution of foreign research and technical advances to our own."[240]

7. In 1952 Charles Chaplin left the United States for a visit abroad. He had been a resident here for forty-one years, and when he left he had in his possession a re-entry permit. Despite these circumstances, James P. McGranery, Attorney General, announced that he might initiate proceedings to prevent Chaplin from coming back to his home in the United States. A re-entry permit, he pointed out, does not assure admission; it merely identifies the holder of the permit. "If he can meet the standards," said the Attorney General, "he will be admitted."[241]

It will be recalled in this connection that the *Chinese Exclusion* case of 1889 involved a Chinese laborer whose reentry was prohibited though he had in his possession a reentry permit. The threat to Chaplin could be made because

act. This act was apparently intended to have only limited application. *Whom We Shall Welcome*, p. 229. The provision in the 1952 act is not limited to time of war or national emergency.

[237] *Whom We Shall Welcome*, 230. [238] *Ibid.*, 232-233.

[239] See memorandum of the Committee in the Appendix.

[240] Report of International Science Policy Group of U.S. Dept. of State, quoted in *op. cit. supra* note 95, p. 213.

[241] *New York Times*, October 3, 1952.

under the law a re-entry, even with a permit, is treated as a new admission, no matter how brief was the visit outside the country (it may have been only to see Niagara Falls from the Canadian side) or how long the alien has lived in this country.

The law should be changed so that a re-entry will no longer be used as an entrapment. A resident alien, if he is permitted to leave the country for a brief visit, ought to be re-admitted without trouble or threats of trouble. If he merits deportation under the law, then he should be deported; but this should be resorted to directly and without subterfuges. The government of the United States is strong enough not to find it necessary to lay snares and traps for the innocent—or guilty—alien.

CHAPTER II

Deportation Policy

IT HAS been pointed out that in thirty-six passages the Pentateuch commands us not to oppress the alien.[1] "This law of shielding the alien from all wrong," Hermann Cohen has said, "is of vital significance in the history of religion. With it alone true religion begins. The alien was to be protected, not because he was a member of one's family, clan, religious community; but because he was a human being. In the alien, therefore, man discovered the idea of humanity."[2] God, said Jeremiah, will permit the people of Israel to dwell in their land only if they meet certain conditions of justice and fair dealing, and one of these conditions was justice to the alien.[3] This, it has been said, "is a conception of nationality, dependent on and in the service of a wider humanity, which has never been surpassed and has still to be realized by the peoples of the world."[4]

Americans are among "the peoples of the world" who have not yet fully realized this Biblical conception of the status of the alien.[5] An alien may find himself the victim of different forms of oppression, e.g., prohibitions upon his

[1] The Talmud; quoted in Jeremiah (H. Freedman, ed., *Soncino Books of the Bible* [London, Soncino Press, 1949], 52).

[2] *Ibid.*, quoting Hermann Cohen.

[3] Jeremiah 7:3-7. [4] Freedman, *loc. cit.*

[5] See generally Konvitz, *The Alien and the Asiatic in American Law.*

entry into certain vocations or professions;[6] perhaps the greatest form of oppression is the ever-present fear of expulsion or deportation.[7] Mr. Justice Jackson has spoken of deportation as a "savage penalty";[8] for often deportation means for the alien that "he is about to begin a life sentence of exile from what has become home, or separation from his established means of livelihood for himself and his family of American citizens."[9] Since there are in the United States some three and a half million aliens,[10] the importance of our deportation policy to them—and to the rest of us—ought to be apparent. We do not mean to imply that all our aliens live under the threat of banishment as under a sword of Damocles; still, because our laws fail to give them vested rights of residence and a substantial measure of constitutional protection should the deportation process be instituted against them, aliens are persons who have been uprooted from their native soil and have no roots in America.[11] It is the deportation policy especially that makes aliens in the United States homeless persons.

DEPORTATION IN AMERICAN HISTORY

The first effort of the American government to deport aliens was made by the Federalist party in 1798. This party, in control of the government, concluded that the country was full of alien spies whose sympathies were favorable to France, and that they were aided and abetted by Thomas

[6] Konvitz, *op. cit.*, ch. vi. [7] *Ibid.*, ch. v.

[8] Jordan v. DeGeorge, 341 U.S. 223 (1951), dis op. at 243.

[9] Justice Jackson, *ibid.*

[10] *The Immigration and Naturalization Systems of the U.S.*, Report of Sen. Com. on Judiciary, Report 1515, 81st Cong., 2d sess. (1950), table on 920. See Note, 66 *Harv. Law Rev.* 643 (1953). See Note by Geo. Kaufmann, 20 *U. of Chicago L. Rev.* 547 (1953).

[11] See Simone Weil, *The Need for Roots* (trans. from French by Arthur Wills; 1952). See review of this book by Isaac Rosenfeld, 19 *Partisan Rev.*, (Sept.–Oct. 1952), 598.

Jefferson and his fellow Republicans. To fight this foreign "menace," those "treasonable ingrates,"[12] the government adopted a number of measures which have become notorious in American history. The Naturalization Act of 1798 raised the residence requirement for naturalization from five to fourteen years. "The purpose of this law," it has been said, "was to make the Republican party wither on the vine by cutting off its supply of foreign born voters. In fact, however, it had no such effect: the Federalists sacrificed their last shred of influence over the foreign vote[13] without materially reducing the strength of the Republican party."[14] The Alien Enemies Act of 1798—the only one of the four acts that was a war measure—provided that in case of war or threatened invasion, the President was to have authority to seize, secure, or remove from the country all resident aliens who were citizens of the enemy nation.[15] The Federalist Congress also enacted the Alien Act of 1798, which authorized the President (John Adams) to expel from the country any alien whom he considered dangerous to the public peace or safety, or whom he believed to be plotting against the country. If we find men in this country, said Harrison Gray Otis, "endeavoring to spread sedition and discord; who have assisted in laying other countries prostrate; whose hands are reeking with blood, and whose hearts rankle with hatred towards us—have we not the power to shake off these firebrands?"[16] The act was to expire in two

[12] See John C. Miller, *Crisis in Freedom: The Alien and Sedition Acts* (1951), quotation on p. 47. See also Ph.D. dissertation, *The Alien and Sedition Laws of 1798,* by James M. Smith (Cornell University, 1951).

[13] The states fixed the qualifications of voters; some of the states had fairly liberal suffrage policies. Miller, *op. cit.,* at p. 48.

[14] *Ibid.,* 47.

[15] *Ibid.,* 50. Cf. the emergency detention provisions of the Internal Security Act of 1950 (McCarran Act). That the Federalist Law was much more severe than the 1950 act, see Miller, *op. cit.,* 52-53.

[16] *Ibid.,* Miller, *op. cit.,* 164.

years. No alien was expelled under its terms; it expired "unhonored and unsung."[17]

Jefferson and Madison made the Alien and Sedition[18] Acts the basis of their Kentucky and Virginia resolutions, in which these Federalist laws were declared to be unconstitutional. In this connection the Kentucky Resolution of 1798, drafted by Jefferson, is of special interest, for Jefferson attacked the Alien Act because it vested in the President the "unconstitutional" power to remove an alien without accusation, without public trail, without confrontation of witnesses, without affording him the right to have witnesses in his favor, without defense, and without counsel.

The acts played a significant part in the defeat of the Federalist party in 1800 and in its final ruin. The popular resentment against the Alien Act was strong because, among other things, it denied the right of trial by jury to a person held for deportation, and because it gave the President judicial powers.[19]

The reasons why Jefferson and other Americans found the Alien Act offensive should be kept in mind when we come to a consideration of current American law and practice with regard to the deportation process.

PLENARY POWER TO DEPORT

The power to deport aliens was not again asserted by Congress until near the end of the 19th century. Having asserted the power to exclude some classes of aliens by legislation adopted in the 1880's, it was logical to enact statutes

[17] *Ibid.*, 193.

[18] There was also the Sedition Act of 1798, a consideration of which at this point would not be relevant. See Miller, *op cit.*, 67, 136, 137, 167, 185, 187, 231.

[19] See Robert E. Cushman, "Alien and Sedition Acts," *Encyc. Soc. Sciences* (1935), I, 635; also W. Anderson, "Enforcement of the Alien and Sedition Laws," *Amer. Hist. Assoc. Annual Rep.* (1912), 113-126.

that would tend to implement the exclusionary policy by providing for the expulsion of illegal entrants. Little by little, however, the process of expulsion, at first used as an incident of the process of exclusion, assumed independent status. Today, legally admitted aliens, as well as illegal entrants, are subject to deportation; but the former, as resident aliens,[20] perhaps have some procedural privileges that are not enjoyed by the latter.

The case that settled the constitutional questions involved in the deportation process was decided by the Supreme Court in 1893. In *Fong Yue Ting v. United States*[21] the court had before it an act of Congress[22] that required all Chinese laborers in the United States who were entitled to remain here to procure a certificate of residence. A person without such a certificate was to be "deemed and adjudged to be unlawfully in the United States," and hence subject to arrest and expulsion. He was to be taken before a federal judge, who was required to order deportation.

A majority of the Supreme Court upheld the act as constitutional. The opinion of Mr. Justice Gray formulated propositions of constitutional law that have been reasserted by the court as recently as 1952. The important points stated by Gray were the following: (1) The right to deport aliens is "absolute" and "unqualified." The admission of an alien creates no obligation on the part of the government; the alien's presence here is a matter of pure permission or simple tolerance. (2) The action of Congress respecting deporta-

[20] For a discussion of the difference between these two classes of aliens, see Louis B. Boudin, "The Settler within Our Gates," 26 *N.Y.U. Law Rev.* (1951), 266-280, 451-474, 634-662. It seems that it was not until 1907 that Congress began to make provision for the deportation of legally resident aliens, thus making deportation independent of the exclusionary process. See Harisiades v. Shaughnessy, note 30 *infra*, footnote 15 in opinion by Justice Jackson.

[21] 149 U.S. 698 (1893). [22] 27 Stat. 25 (1892).

tion is conclusive on the courts; for Congress has the inalienable and inherent right to expel all aliens or any class of aliens, "absolutely or upon certain conditions, in war or in peace." (3) In the exercise of this power Congress may decide to use only executive or administrative agencies; if the use of the courts is not provided for in the legislation, the courts cannot be used. The reason for this is that deportation is not punishment for crime. Due process of law requires judicial process only when a person is charged with the commission of a crime. An alien subject to deportation under statutory provision is not, therefore, entitled to the provisions of the Constitution securing the right of trial by jury, prohibiting unreasonable searches, and prohibiting cruel and unusual punishments.

In several cases decided by the Supreme Court in 1952 these propositions received a stamp of approval. These cases deserve careful consideration.

In *Carlson v. Landon*[23] five aliens were arrested under the Internal Security Act of 1950,[24] each charged with being an alien who was a member of the Communist party. The warrants under which they were arrested directed that they be held in custody pending determination of deportability. They filed petitions for *habeas corpus,* alleging that the detention without bail was in violation of the due process clause of the Fifth Amendment, and of the Eighth Amendment provision that excessive bail shall not be required, nor cruel and unusual punishments inflicted. Carlson showed that he was 39 years of age, came here at the age of six, was married and had two American-born children; Mrs. Stevenson, that she was 45 years of age, has lived here nineteen years, and was married to an American citizen; Hyun, that he was 35 years of age, was taken from Korea to Hawaii at

[23] Carlson v. Landon, and Butterfield v. Zydok, 342 U.S. 524 (1952).
[24] 63 Stat. 987 (1950); 8 U.S.C. (Supp. IV) 137.

an early age and resided there until 1947, when he came to the United States, was married, and had two sons; Carlisle, that he was 55 years of age, and lived in the United States for the past seventeen years; Zydok, that he was 58 years old, had lived here 39 years, has a wife, and has three children and five grandchildren, all native Americans, that his two sons had served in the armed forces of the United States in World War II.[25]

A majority of the court, in an opinion by Mr. Justice Reed, held against the aliens on the constitutional issues. Reed used language that was at least as broad and sweeping as that used by Mr. Justice Gray some sixty years before.

When aliens have come here legally admitted, they have come at the nation's invitation, but, said Reed, "they remain subject to the plenary power of Congress to expel them under the sovereign right to determine what non-citizens shall be permitted to remain within our borders." The power of Congress to deal with aliens, by way of exclusion or deportation, is not based on any delegation of power; Congress deals with aliens as "a sovereign."[26] The power to expel aliens belongs to the political branches of the government—the legislative and the executive; and this power may be exercised entirely through the administrative process, without affording the alien judicial review unless Congress authorizes or permits such review.[27] There is no constitutional right to judicial proceedings or review because "Deportation is not a criminal proceeding and has never been held to be punishment. No jury sits. No judicial review is allowed." Deportation is admittedly "a particularly drastic remedy,"

[25] The years are stated as of 1952.

[26] The court cites for this proposition. U.S. v. Curtiss-Wright Export Corp., 299 U.S. 304 (1936). For discussion of this point see Konvitz, *op. cit.*, 12-20.

[27] The only exception, says the court, is where there is a claim of citizenship, citing Ng Fung Ho v. White, 259 U.S. 276 (1921).

said Reed, and so Congress "has been careful" to provide for a full hearing by an administrative agency, requiring that agency to exercise its responsibility "in a manner consistent with due process."[28]

An alien must be arrested or detained before he can be deported. The Attorney General has been authorized by Congress in his discretion to "hold arrested aliens in custody." Is the Attorney General's "discretion," when he denies bail or bond, subject to judicial review? Since Congress intends that the alien be subject to deportation proceedings that comply with due process, and since detention is a necessary part of these proceedings, it would seem that the courts would have the right and duty to review the denial of bail or bond in order to find whether or not the Attorney General was guilty of a "clear abuse" of discretion.[29] This, apparently, was the line taken by the government, and Reed adopted it. The court concluded that there was no showing in this case of a "clear abuse" of discretion. The Attorney General has a "wide range of discretion," exercised "within the framework of the Subversive Activities Control Act to guard against Communist activities pending deportation hearings."

On the same day that the court decided *Carlson v. Landon*, it also decided *Harisiades v. Shaughnessy*.[30] The case involved three alien Communists who had been ordered deported: Harisiades, 49 years of age, came here when he was

[28] Reed's language seems to mean that this requirement of due process in the administrative hearing is a legislative, not a constitutional, requirement; constitutionally, Congress could, apparently, authorize or require the deportation of aliens without affording a full hearing or due process.

[29] The meaning of Reed's opinion seems to be that judicial review in the interests of due process is a right or duty implied in the expressed intention of Congress; it is legislatively, not constitutionally, given.

[30] Harisiades v. Shaughnessy, Mascitti v. McGrath, Coleman v. McGrath, 342 U.S. 580 (1952).

thirteen years old, and had a wife and two children, all three American citizens. He was a member of the Communist party from 1925 to 1939. A warrant for his deportation because of his membership was issued in 1920 but was not served until 1946. Mascitti, an Italian, was 48 years of age; he came here when he was sixteen. He had an alien wife but their child was American-born. He was a member of the Young Workers party, the Workers party, and the Communist party from 1923 to 1929. Mrs. Coleman was a Russian, 51 years of age, and had been in the United States since she was thirteen. Her husband and three children were American citizens. She was a member of the Communist party at various times, the last time from 1936 to 1937 or 1938. These aliens were ordered deported under the Alien Registration Act of 1940.[31] They contended that since this law was enacted after their membership in the Communist party had terminated, they were not subject to its provisions. In its application to them the act was attacked as unconstitutional because: (1) it deprived them of liberty without due process of law, in violation of the Fifth Amendment; (2) it abridged their freedoms of speech and assembly, in violation of the First Amendment; and (3) it was an *ex post facto* law, which Congress is prohibited to pass.

In his opinion for a majority of the court, Mr. Justice Jackson said that these contentions could not be sustained. Admission for permanent residence confers no vested right on the alien to remain within the country. Constitutionally,[32] the alien is afforded a large measure of economic opportunity;[33] he may invoke the writ of *habeas corpus*;[34] in crim-

[31] 8 U.S.C. 137.
[32] See footnote 9 in Jackson's opinion.
[33] Jackson cites Yick Wo v. Hopkins, 118 U.S. 356 (1886), and Truax v. Raich, 239 U.S. 33 (1915). Cf. Konvitz, *op. cit.*, chs. v, vi, and vii.
[34] Nishimura Ekiu v. U.S., 142 U.S. 651 (1891).

inal proceedings against him he is entitled to the protection of the Fifth and Sixth Amendments;[35] and, unless he is an enemy alien, his property cannot be taken without just compensation.[36] At best, however, his status is ambiguous, and to remain here "is not his right, but is a matter of permission and tolerance." The government has the power to terminate its "hospitality"; his domicile here is held by a "precarious tenure." The power to expel the alien, even after long residence, and even if the practice "bristles with severities," is a power "inherent" in the United States as a sovereign state; "and we leave the law on the subject as we find it." It is true that the expulsion power is being exercised with increasing severity, and it has been said that the point has been reached "where it is the duty of this Court to call a halt upon the political branches of the Government"; but, said Jackson, the answer to this argument must be that "Judicially, we must tolerate what personally we may regard as a legislative mistake." In the present state of the world, said Jackson, "it would be rash and irresponsible to reinterpret our fundamental law to deny or qualify the Government's power of deportation."

As to the argument that the 1940 act was here applied retroactively and was, therefore, an *ex post facto* statute, Jackson said that the *ex post facto* provision in the Constitution forbids only penal legislation that is retroactive in its application. But deportation, "however severe its consequences, has been consistently classified as a civil rather than a criminal procedure."[37]

[35] Wong Wing v. U.S., 163 U.S. 227 (1896).

[36] Russian Volunteer Fleet v. U.S., 282 U.S. 481 (1930).

[37] Harisiades claimed that if he were to get back to Greece, his native country, he would have to face persecution or possible death because of his political views. Poland offered him political asylum, and he elected to go there. He left November 12, 1952, accompanied by his wife and two children, all of whom are American citizens. *New York Times,* November 13, 1952.

Thus, the court in 1952 reaffirmed in all essentials the decision of 1893 in *Fong Yue Ting v. United States.* Today, as two generations ago, "the place to resist unwise or cruel legislation touching aliens is the Congress, not this court."[38]

BASIC FREEDOMS FOR THE ALIEN

The decisions of the Supreme Court in these cases have not remained unchallenged. They have, as a matter of fact, been subjected to strong criticism by outstanding jurists. In the *Fong Yue Ting* case, Justices Brewer and Field and Chief Justice Fuller dissented. In *Carlson v. Landon,* Justices Black and Douglas dissented, as they did also in *Harisiades v. Shaughnessy.*[39] The name of Mr. Justice Murphy should be added to this list for his concurring opinion in *Bridges v. Wixon,* and of Mr. Justice Rutledge for his dissenting opinion in the *Knauer* case.[40] Thus, seven Justices of the Supreme Court have dissented from the propositions that Congress has plenary power to deport aliens and that such aliens are not entitled, in the deportation process, to constitutional protection.

In the first of these cases, involving the deportation of a Chinese national, Mr. Justice Brewer rejected the doctrine of inherent, sovereign powers as "both indefinite and dangerous." The expulsion of a race, or of persons because of their race or birthplace, may be within the inherent powers of a despotism, but no such power was delegated to Congress. Assuming, however, that the power to expel is im-

[38] Frankfurter, conc. op. in Harisiades v. Shaughnessy. Immigration and deportation policies, said Frankfurter, are "wholly outside the power of this court to control," no matter how deeply such policies may offend American traditions. Mr. Justice Clark did not participate in this case.

[39] In Carlson v. Landon, Justices Frankfurter and Burton also dissented but not on constitutional grounds. They construed the 1940 act so as to reach a result opposite to that reached by the majority.

[40] Bridges v. Wixon, 326 U.S. 135 (1945); Knauer v. U.S., 328 U.S. 654 (1946).

plied in one of the express powers of Congress, it can be exercised, said Brewer, only in subordination to limitations and restrictions imposed by the Constitution and not intended for the benefit of citizens only. With regard to the crucial question whether deportation is "punishment," Brewer said: "Deportation is punishment . . . Everyone knows that to be forcibly taken away from home, and family, and friends, and business, and property, and sent across the ocean to a distant land, is punishment; and that oftentimes most severe and cruel." Since deportation deprives a person of liberty and property, the deprivation can be accomplished only according to due process of law. In a deportation proceeding, therefore, concluded Brewer, aliens are entitled to the guarantees of the Fourth, Fifth, Sixth, and Eighth Amendments to the Constitution.

Aliens, according to Mr. Justice Field, differ from citizens only in that they cannot vote[41] or hold public office; but "as men having our common humanity, they are protected by all the guarantees of the Constitution." Like Brewer, Field also rejected the proposition of inherent or sovereign power to deport. Certainly, he said, other nations have asserted the sovereign power to expel: Spain expelled the Moors; England, in the reign of Edward I, expelled 14,000 Jews; France in 1685 drove out the Huguenots; but all these instances, he said, "have been condemned for their barbarity and cruelty, and no power to perpetuate such barbarity is to be implied from the nature of our government, and certainly is not found in any delegated powers under the Constitution . . . I cannot but regard the decision as a blow against constitutional liberty."

Chief Justice Fuller, too, said that no euphemism could disguise the character of deportation as punishment: pun-

[41] Whether or not they can vote is a question decided by state law. See footnote 10 in Jackson's opinion in Harisiades v. Shaughnessy.

ishment without judicial trial. A legally admitted alien is a person whose liberty is protected by the Constitution. Legislation may deprive him of his liberty only if the legislation meets the constitutional tests and only if the deprivation is accomplished by the judicial process and not by the legislation itself.

In the *Bridges* case, before the Supreme Court fifty-two years later, the court set aside the order of deportation, but avoided passing on constitutional issues. Mr. Justice Murphy, however, brought to life the views of Brewer, Field, and Fuller. The assumption that Congress has plenary power to deport aliens is, said Murphy "obnoxious and intolerable" when viewed in the light of our nation's heritage and ideals. Once an alien lawfully enters, "he becomes invested with the rights guaranteed by the Constitution to all people within our borders." Congress may not order the expulsion of aliens because of their race, color, or religion, or because they exercise freedom of political opinion or of association.

In his dissenting opinion in the *Harisiades* case, Mr. Justice Douglas called for a reconsideration of the decision in the *Fong Yue Ting* case, for the decision in that case is "inconsistent with the philosophy of constitutional law which we have developed for the protection of resident aliens." He said:

> An alien, who is assimilated in our society, is treated as a citizen so far as his property and his liberty are concerned. He can live and work here and raise a family, secure in the personal guarantees every resident has and safe from discriminations that might be leveled against him. Those guarantees of liberty and livelihood are the essence of the freedom which this country from the beginning has offered the people of all lands. If those rights, great as they are, have constitutional protection, I think the more important one—the right to remain here—has a like dignity.

The power to deport, said Douglas, is an implied one; but the right to life and liberty is an express right. Why should the implied power be given priority over the express guarantee of the Fifth Amendment? Unless aliens are free from arbitrary banishment, the "liberty" that they enjoy here is "indeed illusory." Banishment "is punishment in the practical sense. It may deprive a man and his family of all that makes life worth while."

This drastic step may at times be necessary in order to protect the national interest. There may be occasions when the continued presence of an alien . . . would be hostile to the safety or welfare of the nation due to the nature of his conduct. But unless such condition is shown, I would stay the hand of the government . . . Congress has not proceeded by that standard. It has ordered these aliens deported not for what they are, but for what they once were.

In his dissenting opinion in *Carlson v. Landon,* Mr. Justice Black agreed with the reasons given by Mr. Justice Douglas in the above opinion why the decision of 1893 should be reconsidered and rejected, and said that the denial of a right to bail under the circumstances was a "shocking disregard" of the following provisions of the Bill of Rights: "Eighth Amendment's ban against excessive bail; First Amendment's ban against abridgment of thought, speech and press; Fifth Amendment's ban against depriving a person of liberty without due process of law."

FAIR HEARING

While the alien detained for deportation is not entitled to a *judicial* hearing or trial, he is constitutionally entitled to a fair hearing. In a case decided in 1950 the Supreme Court stated:

But the difficulty with any argument premised on the proposition that the deportation statute does not require a [fair] hearing, is that without such hearing there would be no constitutional authority for deportation. . . . It was under compulsion of the Constitution that this Court long ago held that an antecedent deportation statute must provide a hearing at least for aliens who had not entered clandestinely and who had been here for some time even if illegally.[42]

In this case the court decided that it was the intention of Congress to subject deportation proceedings to the provisions of the Administrative Procedure Act of 1946,[43] which offered greater procedural protection to the alien than did the procedure of the Immigration and Naturalization Service.[44] Promptly after this decision was announced, Congress passed an act which expressly withdrew application of the Administrative Procedure Act from deportation proceedings.[45] The alien in such proceedings has, as a consequence of this act, rights that the Supreme Court has found to be quite inferior to those given to persons involved in other administrative actions.[46]

In deportation proceedings, what does the constitutional requirement involve? The conditions seem to be that there be reasonable notice, a fair hearing, and an order supported by some evidence.[47] Where these requirements are met, the administrative decision will not be reviewed by the courts.[48]

[42] Wong Yang Sung v. McGrath, 339 U.S. 33 (1950), op. by Justice Jackson. Justices Douglas and Clark did not participate. Justice Reed dissented.

[43] 5 U.S.C. 1001 et. seq; 60 Stat. 237 (1946).

[44] 8 C.F.R. 150. 1 et. seq.

[45] Act of September 27, 1950; 8 U.S.C. 155 (a). The McCarran-Walter Act has left the matter as stated in the text. See *Whom We Shall Welcome,* 159-160.

[46] See annot. in 94 L. Ed. 631, "Construction and Application of Administrative Procedure Act: Federal Cases."

[47] Dis. op. of Justice Douglas in Ludecke v. Watkins, 375 U.S. 160 (1948). As to the right to counsel, see Low Wah Suey v. Backus, 225 U.S. 460 (1912). See annot. in 94 L. Ed. 329, "Due Process in Proceedings to Exclude or Deport Aliens: Supreme Court Cases." See Note, 62 *Yale L. J.* 1000 (1953).

[48] See cases cited, annot. in 94 L. Ed. 329, at p. 333.

The provisions of the Immigration and Nationality Act of 1952 (McCarran-Walter Act)[49] with regard to deportation fall short of the protection afforded by the Administrative Procedure Act, yet seem to meet these constitutional requirements. The act provides that, pending a determination of deportability, an alien may be arrested and may, at the discretion of the Attorney General, be held in custody. The Attorney General's action can be reviewed by a court in a *habeas corpus* proceeding only if there is a "conclusive showing" that the Attorney General is not proceeding "with such reasonable dispatch as may be warranted by the particular facts and circumstances" to determine the aliens' deportability.[50] The deportation proceedings are conducted by a special inquiry officer, who acts as prosecuting attorney and as judge. The alien is to be given reasonable notice as to the charges against him; he may be represented by counsel; and he is to have a reasonable opportunity to examine the evidence against him, to present evidence in his own behalf, and to cross-examine witnesses. The officer's decision to deport must be based on "reasonable, substantial, and probative evidence"; the decision of the Attorney General, however, "shall be final."

The procedure provided by the statute perpetuates evils which the Administrative Procedure Act was designed to cure.[51] Especially obnoxious is the merging of prosecuting and adjudicating functions in the special inquiry officers.[52] Thus it is that constitutionally and legislatively the alien in the United States has failed to achieve the standard of com-

[49] Publ. L. 414, 82d. Cong., 2d. sess. ch. 477; 66 Stat. 163. (1952).

[50] The deportation provisions are in ch. 5 of the act.

[51] See attack on this evil in case cited in note 42 *supra,* 43-44.

[52] Even the Administrative Procedure Act can be said to be "barely an outline of even a minimum of essentials that are basic." R. Parker, "The Administrative Procedure Act: A Study in Overestimation," 60 *Yale Law J.* (1951), 581, 591.

munal protection that was formulated thousands of years ago, before "freedom," "equality," and "democracy" became ideological watchwords. As long as he is subject to deportation upon the order of a single officer, in relation to him we violate the commandment, "And if a stranger sojourn with thee in your land, ye shall not vex him. But the stranger that dwelleth with you shall be unto you as one born among you, and thou shalt love him as thyself."[53]

DENATURALIZATION AS A STEP TOWARD EXPULSION

In the *Harisiades* case Mr. Justice Jackson said that each of the aliens involved in that case had been admitted into the United States "upon passing formidable exclusionary hurdles, in the hope that, after what may be called a probationary period, he would desire and be found desirable for citizenship." The implication in what Jackson said was that naturalization would have served as a haven of refuge and would have placed Harisiades, Mascitti, and Mrs. Coleman beyond the reach of the deportation process. The only safe statement that one can make, however, is that while naturalization makes deportation more difficult, it by no means guarantees continued residence in the United States. If the alien has become naturalized, the government must first denaturalize him before it can deport him as an alien. The government has resorted to denaturalization often enough, so that by now even the public at large should be familiar with the process. On December 10, 1952, the *New York Times* reported on its front page in a double-column headline:

U.S. FILES SUIT AS FIRST STEP
TO DEPORT ALBERT ANASTASIA

The first sentence in this news report read as follows: "The

[53] Leviticus 19:33, 34.

Federal Government began deportation proceedings yesterday against Albert Anastasia, Brooklyn waterfront racketeer and chief executioner of Murder, Inc., by filing suit in Newark, New Jersey, to denaturalize him." The fact that Anastasia had been naturalized in 1943 while serving in the Army, under a special procedure available to members of the armed services, will probably not save him from ultimate deportation as an alien. While it is impossible to shed tears over the sad fate of a racketeer or a Communist, it is necessary to bear in mind that there are over seven million naturalized persons in the United States,[54] who are subject to fears from which the native American is exempt; for the drive against alien and naturalized criminals and Communists must tend to create an atmosphere in which all aliens and all naturalized Americans feel themselves especially vulnerable and exposed. It would be different if there were only one drive; namely, to arrest and prosecute all known racketeers, criminals, and Communists. Alienage and naturalization should certainly not confer any special privileges. But they do confer special disabilities when there are special drives aimed at persons who wear the badge of alienage or naturalization.

That there are special drives against these persons ought to be apparent to anyone who reads the newspapers. Thus, to cite only one or two examples: on October 2, 1952, Attorney General James P. McGranery told a news conference that he had started a drive to take American citizenship from naturalized racketeers, criminals, and Communists, and then to eject them from this country. At this news conference he said he would start denaturalization proceedings against Frank Costello, the gambler, who had obtained citizenship twenty-seven years ago.[55] On June 11, 1951, federal agents

[54] *The World Almanac* (1951), 430. Data are for 1940.
[55] *New York Times,* October 3, 1952.

began a drive to round up aliens, in and around the City of New York, who were suspected of having entered the country illegally. In one month they had rounded up 900 persons. The agents conducted their roundups at hotels, bars, restaurants, homes, the Hoboken docks, and other places.[56]

While the denaturalization and deportation drives go on, there is open toleration of the illegal Mexican immigration, of the "wetbacks" who are solicited to cross the border as cheap laborers in our Southwest. In 1950 our known wetback traffic was between 500,000 and 600,000 persons.[57] "It is remarkable," it has been said, "how some Senators and Representatives who are all for erecting the most rigid barriers against immigration from Southern Europe suffer from a sudden blindness when it comes to protecting the southern border of the United States."[58]

Certainly persons in the United States who violate our laws—our laws against racketeering, gambling, murder, theft, Communist conspiracy—should be prosecuted and punished; but it is nothing short of organized bullying when a particular class—aliens and naturalized citizens—is selected for special treatment. For one thing, such selection for special treatment has the effect of intimidating millions of innocent persons, who become suddenly and keenly aware of their weakness in comparison with native Americans; subjectively they feel themselves to be second-class citizens,[59] or human beings who cannot expect to enjoy freedom from fear. Furthermore, when a drive singles out aliens and naturalized citizens, attention is diverted from the crimes with which they are charged and is concentrated on their char-

[56] *Ibid.*, July 14, 1951.

[57] President's Commission on Migratory Labor, Report: *Migratory Labor in American Agriculture* (1951), 70.

[58] Editorial, *New York Times*, November 28, 1952.

[59] See dis. op. of Judge Edgerton in Lapides v. Clark, 176 F. 2d 619 (1949); cert. den. 94 L. Ed. 527 (1949).

acter as "foreigners," feeding the xenophobia that is latent in human beings. If twenty-seven years after a person has won his citizenship,[60] his naturalization proceedings may be opened for a microscopic examination to discover if perchance the petitioner for naturalization had made a false statement, then the award of citizenship may be only a source of mental anguish; instead of bringing freedom from fear, it opens the door to new worries and fears.

The Immigration and Nationality Act of 1952 makes clear distinctions between the native and naturalized citizens, relegating the latter to an inferior class of citizenship with respect to certain rights and freedoms generally considered fundamental. Thus, a naturalized citizen may have his certificate of citizenship cancelled if within a period of ten years following his naturalization he should refuse to testify as a witness before a congressional committee concerning his subversive activities, and should be convicted of contempt for such refusal;[61] or if he should become a member of or affiliated with a Communist-action organization or some other organization within the terms of the Internal Security Act[62] within five years following his naturalization;[63] or if he should maintain residence for three years in the country of his birth,[64] or for five years in any other foreign country,[65] or if within five years of his naturalization he should go to a foreign country and take up permanent residence there.[66]

Adapting the words of Mr. Justice Black,[67] one may say

[60] See note 55 *supra* concerning Frank Costello. There is no statute of limitations applicable to revocation of naturalization.

[61] Immigration and Nationality Act, sec. 340 (a).

[62] Sec. 25, amending Sec. 305 of the Nationality Act of 1940.

[63] Immigration and Nationality Act, sec. 340 (c).

[64] *Ibid.*, sec. 352 (a) (1). [65] *Ibid.*, sec. 340 (d) (2).

[66] *Ibid.*, sec. 340 (d).

[67] Dis. op. in Carlson v. Landon, 342, U.S. 524 (1952).

that we must have freedom of speech, press, assembly, travel, and protection against compulsory self-incrimination for all or we may eventually have it for none. The indications are, however, that the Constitution, as at present interpreted by the Supreme Court, tolerates these distinctions and the awarding of naturalization upon conditions that deprive the naturalized citizen of freedoms that are guaranteed to all others;[68] and the conditions upon which continued citizenship may depend may be imposed retroactively, without violating the constitutional prohibition against *ex post facto* legislation.[69]

Condemnation of the creation of two classes of citizens has come only from Justices who represent a minority viewpoint. Mr. Justice Murphy said that American citizenship ought not to be a right granted on conditions subsequent. A naturalized citizen, he said, "is not required to imprison himself in an intellectual or spiritual straight-jacket; nor is he obligated to retain a static mental attitude. . . . The naturalized citizen has as much right as the natural born citizen to exercise the cherished freedoms of speech, press and religion."[70] Mr. Justice Rutledge said[71] that under the Constitution there are not two classes of citizens; the only difference between naturalized and other citizens is that the former are ineligible to become President; and statutes ought not to add other differences; no process can take away citizenship for causes or by procedures not applicable alike to native-born and naturalized citizens; Congress, he said, may not create inequalities of status between native-born and naturalized citizens by attaching conditions to the ad-

[68] See case cited in note 59 *supra*.
[69] See this point discussed in Konvitz, *op. cit.*, 118, 119.
[70] Conc. op. in Baumgartner v. U.S., 322 U.S. 665 (1944). See this case and related cases, discussed in Konvitz, *op. cit.*, ch. iv; cf. *op. cit. supra* note 10, pp. 718-19.
[71] Dis. op. in Knauer v. U.S., 328 U.S. 654 (1946).

mission of the latter, to be applied retroactively after naturalization. Citizenship with strings is neither free nor secure. He said:

The act of admission [to citizenship] must be taken as final, for any cause which may have existed at that time. Otherwise, there cannot but be two classes of citizens, one free and secure except for acts amounting to forfeiture within our tradition; the other, conditional, timorous and insecure because blanketed with the threat that some act or conduct, not amounting to forfeiture for others, will be taken retroactively to show that some prescribed condition had not been fulfilled.

If this principle means, said Rutledge, that some or even many disloyal persons cannot be deported, "it is better so than to place so many loyal ones in inferior status. And there are other effective methods for dealing with those who are disloyal, just as there are for such citizens by birth."

A crucial test of the principle stated by Mr. Justice Rutledge is the *Harry Bridges* case, which will go down in American history as a *cause célèbre.* In its span of time, the case, in its various aspects, has been before the American public for some nineteen years, and the *finis* has not yet been written. To discuss the case fully would require a treatise; we shall touch only on the highlights.

THE CASE OF HARRY BRIDGES

The following brief chronology of the case will summarize the main events:

1934:	Agitation begun to deport Bridges, Australian national.
1936:	Special memorandum of three members of the Immigration and Naturalization Service to the Secretary of Labor stating that a review of the evidence and facts showed that there was no legal basis for deportation proceedings.

March 2, 1938: First warrant of arrest issued by Secretary of Labor. Warrant not prosecuted pending Supreme Court decision in *Kessler v. Strecker*.[72]

April 17, 1939: Decision of Supreme Court in *Kessler v. Strecker*. The court held that the federal statute required proof of membership in a proscribed organization at the time of arrest as a basis for deportation. Strecker had been a member of the Communist party but was not one when the warrant in the deportation proceedings was issued; the court held that the warrant must be cancelled.

July 10, 1939: Bridges case heard by Dean James M. Landis, of Harvard Law School, as trial examiner of Labor Department.

December 28, 1939: Dean Landis decided that evidence failed to establish that Bridges was a member of or affiliated with the Communist party at the time the warrant of arrest was issued.

January 8, 1940: Secretary of Labor cancelled warrant of arrest.

May 14, 1940: Bill to deport Bridges introduced in House of Representatives; passed in House later in 1940.[73]

June 14, 1940: Immigration and Naturalization Service taken out of Labor Department and placed in Department of Justice by order of President Roosevelt.

June 28, 1940: Congress amended the law[74] to make past

[72] 307 U.S. 22 (1939).

[73] H. R. 9766, 76th Cong. 3d Sess. (1940).

[74] Alien Registration Act, 54 Stat. 673, 8 U.S.C. 137 (g) (1940): "Any alien who was at the time of entering the United States, or has been at any time thereafter, a member of any one of the classes enumerated in this sec-

	membership in Communist party[75] a basis for deportation.
February 12, 1941:	Second warrant of arrest issued by Attorney General.
March 31, 1941:	Case heard by Judge Charles B. Sears, formerly of New York Court of Appeals, as trial examiner of Department of Justice.
September 26, 1941:	Judge Sears decided that Bridges was subject to deportation.
January 3, 1942:	Board of Immigration Appeals decided that Bridges was not subject to deportation, reversing Judge Sears. The decisions of the Board and of Judge Sears were advisory only. The statute[76] gave finality only to the decision of the Attorney General.
May 28, 1942:	Attorney General Francis Biddle accepted the views of Judge Sears and ordered Bridges deported.[77]
February 8, 1943:	United States District Court dismissed Bridges' petition for writ of *habeas corpus*.[78]
June 26, 1943:	United States Court of Appeals, by 3-2

tion, shall upon the warrant of the Attorney General, be taken into custody and deported." This provision was to be applicable irrespective of the time of the alien's entry into the United States.

[75] The statute does not mention the Communist party. The act speaks of aliens "who believe in, advise, advocate, or teach, or who are members of or affiliated with any organization . . . that believes in, advises, advocates, or teaches: (1) the overthrowing by force or violence of the government of the United States or of all forms of law, or (2) the duty, necessity or propriety of the unlawful assaulting or killing of any officer or officers . . . of the government of the United States. . . , or (3) the unlawful damage, injury, or destruction of property, or (4) sabotage." 8 U.S.C. 137 (c). Sub sec. (d) carries over the definition to aliens who write, publish, circulate, etc., printed matter or written matter that advises, advocates or teaches the overthrow of government, etc.

[76] 8 U.S.C. 155.

[77] Text of ruling in *New York Times,* May 29, 1942.

[78] 49 F. Supp. 292 (1943).

vote, sustained decision of lower court.[79] The majority held that the order of the Attorney General must be sustained if there is discoverable in the record "any evidence" supporting his finding.[80]

June 18, 1945: The Supreme Court, by a 5-3 decision, reversed the judgment against Bridges.[81] The court held that "affiliation" had not been proved. The facts in the case show "little more than a course of conduct which reveals cooperation with Communist groups for the attainment of wholly lawful objectives." Thus, said the court, the deportation order was made for reasons not specified by Congress, which intended that proof of "affiliation" should be of that quality which indicates an adherence to or furtherance of the purposes of the proscribed organization. As to proof of membership in the Communist party, the court held that the finding on this point was based on evidence that was admitted in violation of the rules of the Immigration and Naturalization Service; on the question of membership, therefore, the hearing had been an "unfair hearing."[82]

[79] 144 F. 2d 927 (1944).

[80] Judge Stephens, in his concurring opinion, with which the whole majority of the court agreed, summarized the position of the majority on the sufficiency of the evidence: "In no case have I given the evidence more careful attention than in this one. However, such attention has not left in my mind the pleasurable satisfaction that, barring a very slight possibility of error, the truth has been revealed. Such satisfaction is beside the point here. The simple question this court must answer is: Is there some evidence to sustain the charges? There is."

[81] Bridges v. Wixon, 326 U.S. 135 (1945).

[82] Chief Justice Stone, with Justices Roberts and Frankfurter joining, wrote a dissenting opinion in which he maintained that there was "some" evidence supporting the findings of Sears and Biddle; therefore, the deportation order should be sustained.

September 17, 1945: Bridges was given naturalization papers after swearing that he had never been a Communist.

April 4, 1950: After an 81-day trial in the United States District Court, Bridges was found guilty of perjury. He was convicted for having knowingly made a false statement under oath in his naturalization proceeding.[83] He and his two character witnesses in the naturalization proceeding were also convicted for conspiracy to defraud the United States by having Bridges fraudulently petition for and obtain naturalization.[84] The two witnesses were convicted also for knowingly encouraging, aiding, advising, and assisting Bridges to obtain a certificate of naturalization by fraud.[85] Testimony against Bridges was given by eleven former Communists, who testified that Bridges had attended Communist party meetings from 1933 to 1945.

April 10, 1950: Bridges sentenced to five years imprisonment. His co-defendants were sentenced to two-year prison terms.

June 16, 1950: On the basis of the conviction for perjury and conspiracy, Bridges was ordered denaturalized by the United States District Court.[86]

August 5, 1950: Judge Harris, who had presided at the perjury trial and who had ordered Bridges'

[83] Violation of 18 U.S.C. 371. See 86 F. Supp. 922 (1950).

[84] Violation of 18 U.S.C. 1015 (a). [85] Violation of 18 U.S.C. 1425.

[86] The court acted on the basis of 8 U.S.C. 738. The conviction for perjury, said the court, constituted a conviction for procuring naturalization in violation of law. For the court's opinion see U.S. v. Bridges, 90 F. Supp. 973 (1950).

naturalization papers cancelled, revoked the $25,000 bail on which Bridges was at liberty pending his appeal. The court sustained the contention of the special prosecutor that Bridges' activities are inimical to the security of the United States because of his opposition to American intervention in Korea.[87]

August 24, 1950: After being in jail nineteen days, Bridges was released under bail by a 2-1 decision of the United States Court of Appeals.[88] Judges William Healy and William E. Orr said that his imprisonment "was as startling as it is novel." They said: "A Bridges singled out and jailed by arbitrary judicial action while he is prosecuting with diligence his good-faith appeal poses to our minds a more serious menace to the nation and its institutions than does a Bridges enlarged on bail in accordance with the established rules of law." They asserted that a procedure "admittedly without precedent in the history of the Republic" had been inaugurated in this case; namely, "to make the courts the effective instruments of executive expediency."[89]

September 6, 1952: Court of Appeals upheld convictions for perjury and conspiracy.[90] The court unanimously held that there was "a substantial amount of evidence that Bridges, in fact, joined and became a member of the Communist party." Judge Walter L. Pope said:

[87] *New York Times*, August 6, 1950. [88] *Ibid.*, August 25, 1950.

[89] *Ibid.*; see 184 F. 2d. 881 (1950). Judge Clifton Matthews dissented. He said that Judge Harris had acted "wisely and properly."

[90] Bridges v. U.S., 199 F. 2d 811 (1952).

"Under cross-examination Bridges went on at great length with discourses which, we apprehend, must have caused the jury to wonder whether they were watching a man filled with missionary zeal for expounding views commonly understood to make up the Communist party line, or one who was supremely indifferent to whether he gave the jury the impression that if he was not a Communist party member he must, at any rate, be a fellow traveler."

June 15, 1953: Supreme Court set aside conviction of Bridges and his witnesses on ground that indictment had been barred by three-year statute of limitations.[91]

There are several ways of looking at the case of Harry Bridges. From one point of view a person may be inclined to point to the record of nineteen years of prosecution and say: "Only in a country dedicated to personal freedom would it take the government so many years to deport an alien it deems undesirable. The case demonstrates that Americans, including resident aliens, live under a government of laws, not of men." Looked at from another point of view, the case may be cited as an instance of nineteen years of relentless persecution of a person who would have lost the fight much sooner had he not in back of him a powerful International Longshoremen's and Warehousemen's Union, with a membership of 65,000 workers. The truth probably lies in a combination of both views. In calmer days, I submit, the *Harry Bridges* case will be cited and discussed with apologies. I do not mean to suggest that the California jury,

[91] Reed, Vinson, and Minton dissented; Jackson and Clark did not participate. Bridges v. U.S., 73 S. Ct. 1055 (1953). After the decision, the Department of Justice indicated it would not give up its efforts to deport Bridges. *Christian Science Monitor,* June 16, 1953. There is no statute of limitations regarding denaturalization proceedings.

though it hesitated for some four days to reach a conclusion, was wrong when it found, in effect, that Bridges had been a Communist. In all probability he was a Communist.[92] But Harry Bridges was not alone on trial; it was our administration of justice that was also on trial; and the verdict of history will probably be that, taking the case as a whole, as it extended over a period of nineteen years, it was America, not Harry Bridges, that lost the case.

In 1942, before *Bridges v. Wixon* was decided by the Supreme Court, the *Yale Law Journal* commented on the case in the following language: "To discuss the Bridges case is to write a brief in his behalf. Seldom has an individual in American life been subjected to so relentless a hunt; and so far the law has been one of the most effective weapons at the disposal of Bridges' enemies."[93]

In the Supreme Court Mr. Justice Murphy made the following condemnation of the case:

> The record in this case will stand forever as a monument to man's intolerance of man. Seldom if ever in the history of this nation has there been such a concentrated and relentless crusade to deport an individual because he dared to exercise the freedom that belongs to him as a human being and that is guaranteed to him by the Constitution.[94]

A majority of the Court of Appeals judges, in reversing the order of the trial court which had revoked Bridges' bail, said:

> It is one thing to refrain from interference and quite another for the courts to become themselves the tools of military expedience; and we say now, with all the emphasis we are able to

[92] For good summary of the evidence against Bridges, see *Communist Domination of Certain Unions*, Report of Senate Sub-Committee on Labor and Labor-Management Relations, 82d Cong. 1st sess., Sen. Docum. 89, (1951), 79-96.

[93] 52 *Yale Law Jour.* (1942), 108.

[94] Conc. op. in Bridges v. Wixon, 326 U.S. 135 (1945).

command, that however hard and disagreeable may be the task in times of popular passion and excitement, it is the duty of the courts to set their faces like flint against this erosive subversion of the judicial process.[95]

SENDING THEM BACK AS PARCEL POST

In connection with the Bridges perjury and conspiracy conviction, the policy of deporting alien Communists as advocates of the overthrow of the government by force may be seen "as a reflection of traditional American antipathy for foreign-born radicals. This is compared to relative tolerance of the native-born variety."[96] The pattern has become traditional. In 1798 the fear of a French war led to the adoption of the notorious Alien Acts.[97] Following World War I and the successful Bolskevik Revolution in Russia, a popular delirium spread over the United States, leading to frenzied demands for the deportation of aliens. The frenzy rose to a peak in 1920. Foreigners were associated with "Reds," and "Reds" were associated with illegal conspiracies; *agents provocateurs* were introduced into alien associations; thousands of aliens were arrested, held, and tried without regard for fundamental constitutional safeguards. The detection of crime became the detection of aliens; the prosecution of criminals became the deportation of aliens. Homes were invaded late at night, without warrants; the inmates were taken from their beds and arrested; their rooms were searched; private property was seized; third-degree examinations were common. Public meetings were broken up; audiences were searched, arrested, taken to jail, held without trial or hearing and incommunicado; letters were opened; persons arrested were deprived of counsel. It was

[95] 184 F. 2d. 881 (1950).
[96] Robert R. Brunn, "Bridges Trial in Retrospect: Was World Communism Star Witness?" *Christian Science Monitor,* April 18, 1950.
[97] *Op. Cit. supra* note 12.

a real "head-hunting jamboree." When the Department of Labor, thanks to Louis F. Post, Assistant Secretary, would not permit itself to be stampeded, the Department of Justice (A. M. Palmer was then Attorney General) denounced the Department of Labor as sympathetic to lawless agitators. A group of prominent lawyers, with Dean Roscoe Pound at their head, publicly condemned the Department of Justice for its lawlessness in connection with the deportation crusade. This committee made six charges: (1) third degree tortures were inflicted; (2) arrests were made without warrants; (3) there were unreasonable searches and seizures; (4) the government used *agents provocateurs;* (5) the government compelled aliens to be witnesses against themselves; (6) the Attorney General had misused his office.[98]

Following World War II, an anti-alien atmosphere became apparent. It did not by any means assume the ugly proportions of the "Palmer-Raids"; it is doubtful if a Pound investigation would uncover acts as monstrous as those summarized above. But there has been a drive to deport undesirable aliens and to revoke naturalization papers, with the result that aliens and foreign-born Americans find themselves living in a subdued fear of what may be done to them.

When in 1952 the New York State Crime Commission investigations disclosed the details of the waterfront racket, relatively little was threatened against native-born criminals, perhaps because if they were indicted and tried, they might name names, even big names, and implicate public officials, including judges, whom they helped place in office. Deportation, however, can be accomplished much more quietly. It was announced that the federal government had begun

[98] Post, *Deportation Delirium of 1920* (1923). See also Colyer v. Skeffington, 265 F. 17 (1920); Skeffington v. Katzeff, 277 F. 129 (1922); Ex parte Jackson, 263 F. 110 (1920).

deportation proceedings against Albert Anastasia, who had been naturalized nine years before while serving in the Army;[99] similar action was started against Vito Genovese, who became a citizen in 1936.[100] Proceedings against these gangsters and racketeers to denaturalize and then to deport them involve small risks to public officials and other respectable citizens; such proceedings help take the heat off government agencies responsible for the enforcement of the criminal law. These foreign-born criminals have served their purpose, and now they can be sent back where they came from, without regard to the fact that they may have come here as young children, lost their innocence of childhood, and acquired their criminal propensities and skills in this country, and that morally we, and not their native countries, may need to share with them responsibility for their characters and actions.

A spokesman for the Italian Foreign Office has said that his country would bar the entry of Italian-born racketeers who may be deported, after denaturalization proceedings, by the United States. He said:

> We do not want another Lucky Luciano. He lived in Italy a short time and then spent most of his time in the United States. Now we have to pay for him. It's not blood that makes a man delinquent; it's society. . . . They can't send them back like parcel post. . . . If they send these people back to us, they won't be permitted to land.[101]

Certainly foreign-born criminals are not exempt from our criminal laws; but this is precisely the point: they are not being prosecuted for their crimes; instead, they are being deported because they are aliens; thus they are exempted from prosecution for breaking our criminal laws, and their

[99] *New York Times*, December 10, 1952.
[100] *Ibid.*, November 22, 1952.
[101] *Ibid.*, January 2, 1953.

deportation serves as a screen behind which the native-born variety of criminal may continue his nefarious trade.

In the long run these drives against aliens and foreign-born citizens have an evil effect on the administration of justice. The denial of bail to Harry Bridges was not a singular occurrence. It was on August 24, 1950, that the Court of Appeals ordered Bridges released under bail, reversing the order of Judge Harris. Yet, several months later, on November 17, 1950, Judge Sylvester J. Ryan, of the United States District Court in New York, found it necessary to conclude that sixteen aliens detained at Ellis Island had been denied bail, and that the denial "was arbitrary and an abuse of discretion on the part of the Attorney General." These aliens, Judge Ryan pointed out, had been resident in this country for some years, some of them for many years; many of them were married to American citizens and had raised families in this country.[102]

In the summer of 1951, Senator Pat McCarran, himself the son of immigrant parents, warned that there may be five million aliens illegally here, including "militant Communists, Sicilian bandits and other criminals" in vast numbers. Commenting on this "spine-tingling" statement, the *New York Times* said:

> There certainly are illegal aliens in this country, and probably they include some Communists, some bandits (whether Sicilian or not) and unquestionably a great many Mexican "wetbacks." They should be thrown out. But neither Mr. McCarran nor anyone else knows how many there are and such hair-raising statements as he has just made serve no valid purpose, tend to feed all the latent fears and prejudices that ought to have been buried with the Know-Nothings a hundred years ago and becloud the real problem of protecting our country against subversives, both alien and native-born. Of course we must be on guard against

[102] *Ibid.*, November 18, 1950.

dangerous aliens; but, as Mr. McCarran might do well to recall, some of our more famous bandits as well as more notorious foreign agents have been 100 percent home grown.[103]

It is not only our law enforcement agencies that are responsible for the plight of our aliens and foreign-born citizens. Congress, notably in the Alien Registration Act of 1940, in the Internal Security Act of 1950, and in the Immigration and Nationality Act of 1952 (not to mention the acts that followed World War I),[104] has placed aliens and naturalized citizens in a vulnerable position and one that invites trouble for them. The Supreme Court also needs to share responsibility for its refusal to adopt the position of Justices Brewer, Field, Fuller, Murphy, Rutledge, Black, and Douglas, the essence of which is that the Bill of Rights protects the alien (at least the resident, legally-admitted alien)[105] as fully as it does the citizen; that deportation should be assimilated to punishment for crime, so that the alien held for deportation may have the same guarantees of constitutional freedoms and rights as those which the Constitution affords to native-born criminals; that the Constitution does not recognize two classes of citizens, the native-born and the naturalized, one type free and secure, the other subject to conditions subsequent. Until the Supreme Court undoes the mischief of its decision in *Fong Yue Ting v. United States,*[106] deportation, and denaturalization as a step towards its achievement, will be fairly easy of accomplishment—that is, unless one has the resources of a Harry Bridges.

"In America," an observant British writer has said, "unique as far as I know among the nations of the Western

[103] Editorial, August 24, 1951. [104] See Konvitz, *op. cit.*, 60.
[105] Louis B. Boudin, "The Settler Within Our Gates," 26 *N.Y.U. Law Rev.* (1951), 266, 451, 634.
[106] 149 U.S. 698 (1893).

World, 'stranger' is not hostile but a friendly form of address. The American expects and welcomes curiosity!"[107] This is probably true except in times of stress, when latent fears and prejudices come to the surface and tend to give us a devil of a time by leading us to sin against our own better nature. Times of stress put a strain on the Bill of Rights as well as on citizens; but we should bear in mind that, "when those hard won guarantees of the Bill of Rights are stretched or strained—even in the cause of national security—the road back may be hard to find."[108]

It is not to be inferred from what has been said that our millions of foreign-born live in a virtual state of siege. Nothing could be further from the truth. Yet, the drives conducted against alien and naturalized Communists and criminals must tend to intimidate all foreign-born persons in the United States. Certainly, this effect is an unintended byproduct of the government's policies; but policies that will have dismaying effects on millions of innocent persons, though intended to reach only relatively few, ought not to be adopted by the government of a free and democratic nation, dedicated to life under the rule of law. There are established, defined, civilized procedures available to the government for dealing with persons, foreign-born or native-born, who violate our criminal laws. Backed by these laws, our government should find itself sufficiently strong to deal with conspirators and gangsters. As long as the government will by-pass these laws, which can reach all persons, foreign-born and native-born alike, and resort to methods intended to reach only the foreign-born persons in our country, it will be open to charges of bad faith and injustice.

[107] D. W. Brogan, "Why Americans and British Don't Understand One Another," *The English Speaking World* (December 1952), 17.

[108] Editorial, "Ends and Means," concerned with the Bridges Case, *Christian Science Monitor*, August 19, 1950.

CONCLUSION

Dissenting in a recent case, in which the United States Court of Appeals upheld an order of deportation, Judge Charles E. Clark said, "I recognize that the area in which an alien can seek judicial relief and does not remain subject to the unreviewable and uncontrollable doom of a governmental official is being steadily narrowed by Congress."[109] The doom of deportation is one against which our courts have protested time and again, in an effort to awaken the conscience of Congress or the public, but thus far success has come exclusively to the side that represents harshness, and even cruelty, in the treatment of aliens. If Congress should want to introduce some measure of humanity in such treatment, the necessary reforms can be pointed out easily.

[109] U.S. ex rel. Dolenz v. Shaughnessy, 200 F. 2d 288 (1952).

On February 9, 1953, the Supreme Court decided the case of Chew v. Colding, 73 S. Ct. 472. The case involved a Chinese seaman who was admitted to permanent residence in the United States in 1945. In World War II he served with credit in the Merchant Marine. He never had any difficulties with the government. In 1950 he left aboard a vessel as a chief steward. When he returned in 1951 the immigration inspector at San Francisco ordered him temporarily excluded as an alien whose entry was deemed prejudicial to the public interest. In a *habeas corpus* proceeding the Supreme Court held that while the Ellen Knauff case involved an alien entrant, this case involved a resident alien, and that resident aliens, when they are in the United States, have a right to be heard; they have a right to procedural due process. They may be expelled and deported, but before their expulsion they are entitled to notice of the nature of the charge and a hearing at least before an executive or administrative tribunal. They must be given a fair opportunity to be heard. They must be given an opportunity to prove, e.g., mistaken identity. Petitioner's voyage did not terminate these rights. For the purposes of his constitutional rights, with respect to procedural due process, the court assimilated petitioner's status to that of an alien who had not physically left the United States. Justice Minton was a lone dissenter.

The case should be compared with the Mezei case, decided in the following month, and discussed in Chapter I, note 144. The Court distinguished the Mezei case from the Chew case by saying that in the former case the alien apparently had not in his possession reentry papers when he left the United States; also, that Mezei was gone 19 months, while Chew only 4 months. Mezei could be excluded without a hearing, while Chew was entitled to a hearing.

1. Deportation hearings should be made to conform with the requirements of the Administrative Procedure Act. As we have seen, the Supreme Court at one time assumed that this had been done by Congress,[110] but new legislation[111] quickly changed the picture adversely to the interests of the alien.

In view of the gravity of deportation and its consequences to the alien and his family (which may consist of American citizens), there ought to be substantial judicial review of deportation orders.[112]

2. The law with regard to bail in deportation proceedings should be liberalized. A denial of bail, considering all the facts in a case, may be unreasonable, and should be illegal, despite the fact that the Attorney General may be proceeding with "reasonable dispatch."

In connection with this question of bail, Congress should give serious consideration to some of the cases that have recently come before the federal courts in which the government attorneys sought to hold aliens under arrest without bail. The following set of facts will serve as an illustration of a procedure that is all too common.

Antonia Sentner came to the United States from Croatia in 1914 when she was eight years old. She has resided in the United States ever since. She was educated in the public and parochial schools of this country. She married and raised a family: one married daughter (to whom three children have been born), and two younger children (aged twelve and eight) who resided with their mother. Until 1949 the government made no effort to move against her. Then she was arrested in proceedings for her deportation; she was placed under bail. Over a year passed and no hear-

[110] Wong Yang Sun v. McGrath, 339 U.S. 33 (1950); modified at 908.

[111] *Whom We Shall Welcome*, 159-160.

[112] See Heikkila v. Barber, 73 S. Ct. 603 (1953). *Cf.* Note, 62 *Yale L. J.* 1000 (1953)

ing was held. Following passage of the Subversive Activities Control Act of 1950, she was again arrested. The United States District Court judge found that during the year since the warrant had been issued in 1949, she had kept herself available at all times for any hearing and complied with the terms of the bail bond. Despite these facts the government attorneys took her into custody, placed her in jail, and told the court that she will stay in jail "pending final determination of deportation proceedings" against her. The alien's affidavit showed that she had been living at the same address in St. Louis since 1942, with her husband, two minor children, her father, her invalid mother, and her mother-in-law, that she had no domestic help and that there was no one else capable of maintaining the household and caring for the children and her invalid mother. The judge had difficulty in believing that her presence within the community constituted a danger to public safety or security, and held that she was entitled to bail.[113]

3. Under the act of 1952 an alien is subject to deportation at any time. The President's Commission recommended that no alien be held subject to deportation more than ten years after the violation has occurred. Even ten years is a long period of time—an alien may build up a home and a business within this period, and his deportation may hurt innocent people. The statutory period of limitations recommended by the Commission is the least that Congress should provide. The absence of such a limitations period, as we have seen, leads to the deportation of aliens after they have spent as much as twenty or thirty years in the United States —a patently inhumane law.

4. Deportation should again become an adjunct of the exclusion process and limited to this function. If an alien

[113] Ex parte Sentner, 94 F. Supp. 77 (1950). *Cf.* Carlson v. Landon, 342 U.S. 524 (1952); Yaris v. Esperdy, 108 F. Supp. 735 (1952).

obtains his admission by a willful and material fraud, he should be subject to deportation (within the ten year period of a statute of limitations); otherwise, if his entry was legal, he should be exempt from deportation. If he should commit any crime or act of subversion, he should be made subject to the same law that applies to the citizens: "Ye shall have one manner of law, as well for the stranger, as for one of your own country: for I am the Lord your God."[114] Equal justice means equality of treatment, under the same law—one which respects neither the rich nor the native-born more than the poor or the foreigner.

5. Denaturalization should be suffered only for willful and material fraud in procuring naturalization papers. Conduct subsequent to naturalization should not open the door to loss of citizenship. A ten-year statute of limitations for denaturalization, recommended by the President's Commission, should be enacted. All marks of difference between native-born and naturalized citizens, beyond the constitutional one, should be eliminated from our laws, so that there may be no suggestion of second-class or inferior citizenship for any one in American society.

[114] Leviticus 24:22.

CHAPTER III

Becoming a Citizen

THE CONSTITUTIONAL Convention of 1787 avoided a definition of citizenship. The Constitution provided only that the citizens of each state shall be entitled to all privileges and immunities of citizens in the several states,[1] and that Congress shall have the power to establish a uniform rule of naturalization.[2] The Convention acted, however, on the assumption that there would be natural-born citizens[3] and naturalized citizens.

CITIZENSHIP BY BIRTH

According to the English common law a person became a natural-born subject of the king by birth within the king's domain. It was assumed that this *jus soli* of the common law applied in the United States.[4] As a consequence of the decision of the Supreme Court in the *Dred Scott*[5] case in 1857 and of the Civil War, the question as to who are native-born citizens received constitutional clarification.

In his opinion for the majority of the court in the *Dred Scott* case, Chief Justice Taney said that the question before

[1] Art. IV, sec. 2. [2] Art. I, sec. 8, cl. 4.

[3] "No person except a natural born citizen . . . . shall be eligible to the office of the President." Art. II, sec. 1, cl. 5.

[4] Munro v. Merchant, 26 Barb. (N.Y.) 383 (1858).

[5] Scott v. Sandford, 19 How. (U.S.) 393 (1857).

the court was "simply this": "Can a Negro, whose ancestors were imported into this country, and sold as slaves, become a member of the political community formed and brought into existence by the Constitution of the United States, and as such become entitled to all the rights, privileges, and immunities, guaranteed by that instrument to the citizen?" The Supreme Court held that Negroes who had been imported as slaves, and their descendants, "whether they had become free or not," were not part of the "people of the United States" who, according to the Preamble to the Constitution, ordained and established the Constitution for the United States. Whether slave or free, Negroes "had no rights which the white man was bound to respect." They were not citizens of the United States, not only because they were or had been slaves, but also because "Negroes in the United States were as a whole a degraded people who had not been generally accepted as a part of the body of citizens."[6]

Immediately after the Civil War, Congress attempted to undo the substance of the decision of the Supreme Court by passing an act according to which all persons born in the United States, and not subject to any foreign power, excluding Indians not taxed, were declared to be citizens of the United States.[7] Two years later the Fourteenth Amendment was declared adopted. It provided that "All persons born or naturalized in the United States, and subject to the jurisdiction thereof, are citizens of the United States and of the state wherein they reside."[8] This provision put at rest the question of citizenship generally, though its main purpose was to establish the citizenship of the Negro.[9]

[6] C. B. Swisher, *American Constitutional Development* (1943), 244. It should be remembered that Justices McLean and Curtis dissented in the *Dred Scott* case.

[7] 14 Stat. 27 (1866). See discussion of this act in Konvitz, *The Constitution and Civil Rights* (1947), 4.

[8] Amendment 14, sec. 1.

[9] Slaughter House Cases, 16 Wall. (U.S.) 36, 72-73. See also Strauder v.

The object of the qualifying words, "and subject to the jurisdiction thereof," was to exclude children of diplomatic representatives of a foreign state, and children born of alien enemies in hostile occupation.[10]

With regard to the citizenship of Indians, the decision of the Supreme Court in *Elk v. Wilkins*[11] in 1884 accomplished the same result as that which the *Dred Scott* decision had accomplished with regard to the citizenship of Negroes. The Supreme Court was presented with the question whether or not the Fourteenth Amendment declared Indians, born in the United States and not subject to tribal jurisdiction, citizens of the United States and of the states wherein they resided. The case involved an Indian who had separated himself from his people and was living among white people in Omaha. The court held that he was not a citizen. Indian tribes, the court said, were alien nations, with whom the President and the Senate made treaties; Indians were not part of the people of the United States; they were in a dependent condition; in relation to the government, they were in a state resembling that of the relationship between ward and guardian. Indians, said the court, can become citizens only by naturalization; that is, if Congress will pass special legislation granting them this privilege, or if treaties should accord them this privilege, but not otherwise.

In a dissenting opinion Mr. Justice Harlan[12] contended that it was the intention of the Fourteenth Amendment to confer citizenship upon Indians who were living outside Indian reservations. There were many Indians, he said, who "were as fully prepared for citizenship as were or are

---

West Virginia, 100 U.S. 303 (1880); Elk v. Wilkins, 112 U.S. 94 (1884).

[10] U.S. v. Wong Kim Ark, 169 U.S. 649, 682 (1898).

[11] 112 U.S. 94 (1884).

[12] Justice Woods also dissented.

vast numbers of white and colored races in the same localities." Is it conceivable, he asked,

that the statesmen who framed, the Congress which submitted, and the people who adopted that amendment, intended to confer citizenship, national and state, upon the entire population in this country of African descent. . . , and . . . to exclude from such citizenship Indians who had never been in slavery, and who, by becoming *bona fide* residents of states and territories within the complete jurisdiction of the United States had evinced a purpose to abandon their former mode of life and become a part of the people of the United States?

Despite the Fourteenth Amendment, said Harlan, there is still in this country

a despised and rejected class of persons, with no nationality whatever; who, born in our territory, owing no allegiance to any foreign power, and subject, as residents of the states, to all the burdens of government, are yet not members of any political community nor entitled to any of the rights, privileges, or immunities of citizens of the United States.

As a result of this decision of the court in 1884, Indians born in the United States were not American citizens, though capable of naturalization by treaty or special law. Three years later an act of Congress accorded citizenship to certain Indians, including those who had left their tribes and adopted the ways of civilization.[13] In 1919 an act of Congress granted the privilege of becoming citizens to Indians who had served in the armed forces of the United States in World War I.[14] Finally, in 1924, an act of Congress went all the way to undo the Supreme Court's decision of 1884. It provided that all Indians born in the United States were to be citizens.[15]

[13] 24 Stat. 388 (1887).

[14] 41 Stat. 350 (1919). See generally Felix S. Cohen, *Handbook of Federal Indian Law* (2 vols., 1941, 1942).

[15] 43 Stat. 253 (1924). There were about 125,000 Indians who were

Indians, then, are now citizens of the United States by birth (*jus soli*). But unlike members of the white and Negro races (and other races as well, as we shall see), citizenship by birth is enjoyed by Indians as a privilege extended by acts of Congress[16] and not as a right provided by the Constitution. They are citizens not through naturalization, and not by virtue of the Fourteenth Amendment, but by special congressional action.[17]

What of members of other races born in the United States? Such persons faced less difficulty in the Supreme Court than did the Negro or the Indian. In 1898 the Supreme Court, in *United States v. Wong Kim Ark*,[18] held that a child born in the United States of Chinese parents was an American citizen from the time of his birth. This decision was reached at a time when laws of Congress excluded Chinese persons from settling in the United States or acquiring American citizenship. The court said that the exclusionary policies of Congress could not cut down the effectiveness of the Fourteenth Amendment. The sweep of this decision was such as to cover persons born in the United States of Japanese parents or members of other races or nations affected by the exclusionary policies of Congress.[19] There are today,

directly affected by this act. *Yearbook on Human Rights for 1948* (United Nations, 1950), 403.

[16] Sec. 201 of the Nationality Code of 1940; 8 U.S.C. 601.

[17] It may be, of course, that if the question were presented to the Supreme Court, the decision might now be that Indians are "subject to the jurisdiction" of the United States and are, therefore, by force of the Fourteenth Amendment, natural-born citizens. Cf. Ex parte Green, 123 F. 2d 862 (1941); cert. den. 316 U.S. 668 (1941). For all practical purposes native-born Indians—as well as members of other aboriginal peoples—are native-born citizens of the United States and of the states wherein they reside. 8 U.S.C. 601 (1940).

[18] 163 U.S. 228; Chief Justice Fuller and Justice Harlan dissented.

[19] Regan v. King, 49 F. Supp. 222; aff'd 134 F. 2d 413 (1943); cert. den. 319 U.S. 753 (1943).

then, no racial disability laws standing in the way of a person born in the United States acquiring citizenship at birth.

By acts of Congress persons born within certain territories also acquire American citizenship at birth. This is true of persons born in Puerto Rico, Alaska, Hawaii, the Virgin Islands, and Guam.[20] In 1940 over 91 per cent of all persons residing in the United States and these territories[21] were native-born citizens.[22]

CITIZENSHIP THROUGH NATURALIZATION

Immediately after the Constitution was adopted Congress passed a naturalization act. This act of 1790[23] granted the right to claim citizenship under specified conditions to all *free white* aliens. The first exception to this rule of exclusiveness on the part of the white race with regard to citizenship through naturalization was an act of 1870, by which aliens of African descent became eligible for naturalization.[24] The next exception was not made until seventy years later (1940), when, in furtherance of our "Good Neighbor Policy," the class of eligibles was opened up to include "descendants of races indigenous to the Western Hemisphere."[25] In 1943 Chinese were made eligible for naturalization,[26] and in 1946 Filipinos and people indigenous to India were accorded the same privilege.[27] The Immigration and Nationality Act of 1952 wiped out all racial bars on naturalization. This law provides that the "right of a

[20] Nationality Code of 1940, 8 U.S.C. 601, 602; Immigration and Nationality Act of 1952, secs. 301, 302, 304, 305, 306, 307.

[21] Except Guam.

[22] *The Immigration and Naturalization Systems of the United States*, Senate Report 1515, 81st Cong., 2d sess. (1950), 685. See Note, 66 *Harv. L. Rev.* 643 (1953).

[23] 1 Stat. 103 (1790). [24] 16 Stat. 254 (1870).

[25] Nationality Code of 1940, 8 U.S.C. 703 (1940).

[26] 57 Stat. 600 (1943). [27] 60 Stat. 416 (1946).

person to become a naturalized citizen of the United States shall not be denied or abridged because of race."[28]

Prior to the passage of these acts from 1940 to 1952, the following persons had been declared ineligible for naturalization:[29] Chinese, Japanese, Hindus, Afghans, Burmese, Koreans, Maoris, Polynesians, Samoans, and Filipinos.[30] As to Mexicans, Parsees, and Arabs, there was a conflict of authorities. It is apparent from this list that not only "race," but also "color" served as a disqualification.[31] Fortunately, however, this has become a matter of history. It took from 1790 to 1952 to eliminate the racial or color bar to naturalization. The important thing to bear in mind is that it has been wiped out. The Special Subcommittee to Investigate Immigration and Naturalization, which sponsored the McCarran-Walter Bill, reported:

The evidence and testimony presented to the subcommittee are overwhelmingly in favor of the removal of racial bars to naturalization. It is important to note that racial prejudices have decreased radically in the last quarter of a century in the communities where most of those who are racially ineligible live. The hysteria and fears of the war years have died down.[32]

[28] Sec. 311.

[29] The authorities are collected and analyzed in Konvitz, *The Alien and the Asiatic in American Law* (1946), 79-97. It should be noted that the exclusion of Chinese aliens from naturalization was not left to judicial interpretation. 23 Stat. 115 (1870).

[30] Filipinos were eligible if they had served in the armed forces of the United States. 8 U.S.C. 703; Konvitz, *op. cit. supra* note 29, p. 96; also *op. cit. supra* note 22, p. 695.

[31] See discussion of this point in Konvitz, *op. cit. supra* note 29, pp. 88 ff.

[32] *Op. cit. supra* note 22, p. 697. It may be noted that of all national groups, only the Chinese were excluded from the privilege of naturalization by an express statutory provision. "No state court or court of the United States shall admit Chinese to citizenship." 22 Stat. 61 (1882). Other nationals were excluded because they were not "white persons," or "persons of African nativity or descent," or "descendants of races indigenous to the Western Hemisphere." 54 Stat. 1140, 8 U.S.C. 703 (1940).

INELIGIBILITY BECAUSE OF OPINION

It is of interest to note that as ineligibility because of race or color was gradually, and in 1952 absolutely, eliminated, ineligibility because of opinion became a more prominent feature of our naturalization process. The exclusionary emphasis shifted from racial to ideological considerations. This shift was typical of events generally in the 1940's and 1950's—a widespread conviction that a democracy ought equally not to tolerate racial policies which lead to prejudice and discrimination *and* subversive policies which lead to a weakening of our political and social institutions in such a way as to prepare us for conquest by a foreign power or by a totalitarian ideology. The racial test was a relatively simple one; one could understand its scope and meaning, and attack or defend the test as just or unjust, expedient or inexpedient, desirable or dangerous.[33] It is quite different with matters of opinion, belief and loyalty.[34] In the past—until a decision of the Supreme Court in 1946—it was persons with religious or conscientious scruples against bearing arms who had difficulty with the naturalization process; today—following especially the enactments of the Internal Security Act of 1950 and the Immigration and Nationality Act of 1952—it is Communists and fellow-travelers.

PACIFISM

For years the courts denied conscientious objectors naturalization certificates because, it was held, persons who would not be willing to serve in the military forces of the

[33] Now and then, of course, the absurdity of the racial or color test became apparent; see U.S. v. Thind, 261 U.S. 204 (1922) and discussion of this case in Konvitz, *op. cit. supra* note 29, ff. 88 ff.

[34] Witness the Harry Bridges perjury and conspiracy trial, which lasted over eighty court days and the record of which is in over two million words, many of them devoted to ideological discussions.

United States could not take, without mental reservations, the oath to support and defend the Constitution.[35]

In the first notable case involving a conscientious objector, the case of *Rosika Schwimmer*, naturalization had been denied to a woman fifty years of age who had testified at her naturalization proceedings that she was a pacifist and would not bear arms. The Supreme Court in 1929 upheld the denial.[36] Two years later the court upheld the denial of citizenship to a Baptist minister and professor of divinity at Yale, whose position was that he would bear arms only if he concluded that the war was morally justified. He said that he would never put allegiance to government before allegiance to the will of God. The court held that he, too, had failed to establish his attachment to the principles of the Constitution.[37]

These decisions were widely condemned.[38] It was pointed out that the source of the trouble was not a constitutional or even a statutory provision, but a question on one of the forms of petition for citizenship, which read as follows: "If necessary, are you willing to take up arms in defense of this country?" This question had been introduced in 1922 by an administrator upon the request of "patriotic" groups.

The oath of allegiance is statutory. It affirms a willingness to "bear true faith and allegiance to the Constitution." This language, while appropriate to impress the moral sense and conscience, cannot be subjected to minute and logical analysis; its meaning is far from precise. For an

[35] For the oath, see 8 U.S.C. 735 (1940).

[36] Schwimmer v. U.S., 279 U.S. 644 (1929). Justice Holmes wrote one of his notable dissenting opinions, in which he was joined by Justices Brandeis and Sanford. For fuller discussion of this case, and other cases involving naturalization of pacificists, see Konvitz, *op. cit. supra* note 29, 97 ff.

[37] Macintosh v. U.S., 283 U.S. 605 (1931). Justices Hughes, Holmes, Brandeis, and Stone dissented.

[38] See Konvitz, *op. cit. supra* note 29, p. 101, note 53 for references.

administrative official to reduce this language to the sense of a willingness to bear arms is to reduce the essentially indefinable to a definition. To do this was to go beyond the expressed will of Congress by adding qualifications for naturalization that depend on the views of the examining officials, rather than on the intentions of Congress. Furthermore, the policy of Congress, as expressed in the selective service and training acts, was to give special consideration to conscientious objectors. The exclusion from naturalization of conscientious objectors implies a distinction between native-born and naturalized citizens, the constitutionality of which may be questioned.[39]

In 1946 the Supreme Court overruled its prior decisions. In the *Girouard* case[40] the court adopted the dissenting opinions of Justices Holmes and Hughes in the earlier cases and held that nothing in the act of Congress makes a promise to bear arms a prerequisite to naturalization, and the court ought not to assume that Congress implied such a promise. Refusal to bear arms is not necessarily a sign of disloyalty or an indication of lack of attachment to our institutions, said the court; furthermore, the bearing of arms is not the only way in which the country may be defended and supported. The essence of the decision was that this is a matter for Congress and that the will of Congress should be expressed by a legislative act.

The intention of Congress is no longer obscure. The Immigration and Nationality Act of 1952[41] provides that a person, in order to be admitted to citizenship, shall take an oath to support and defend the Constitution, to bear true faith and allegiance to the United States, and, when re-

[39] Cf. Lapides v. Clark, 176 F. 2d 619 (1949); cert. den. 70 S. Ct. 101 (1949) rearg. den. 70. S. Ct. 187 (1949).

[40] Girouard v. U.S., 328 U.S. 61 (1946). Justices Stone, Frankfurter, and Reed dissented.

[41] Sec. 337 (a).

quired by law, to bear arms, or to perform work of national importance under civilian direction, or to perform noncombatant service in the Armed Forces of the United States.

The alternatives to the bearing of arms are available only to persons who are conscientious objectors "by reason of religious training and belief," which the law defines as "an individual's belief in a relation to a Supreme Being involving duties superior to those arising from any human relation, but does not include essentially political, sociological or philosophical views or a merely personal moral code."[42] This definition gives legal recognition to the claim of the Yale divinity professor who was denied naturalization when he asserted that he would not put allegiance to government before allegiance to the will of God; to the claim that there may be times when rendering unto God may make impossible rendering unto Caesar. It is probably the first express statutory statement that in a conflict between conscience and governmental command, the latter should give way.

It should be stated, however, that no constitutional principle is involved. The statutory recognition of conscientious objection to bearing arms is a matter of congressional grace.[43] The Constitution[44] authorizes Congress to establish a uniform rule of naturalization, but this power of Congress, the Supreme Court has said, "is not trammeled, and it may grant or withhold the privilege of naturalization upon any grounds or without any reason as it sees fit."[45] Thus, with regard to naturalization, as with immigration and de-

[42] The Internal Security Act of 1950, sec. 29, also amended sec. 335 of the Nationality Code of 1940, with regard to the oath of allegiance; the 1952 amendment, however, went further in recognizing conscientious scruples. The term "religious training and belief" is defined only in the 1952 act. Nor is the term defined in the Selective Training and Service Act of 1940, 54 Stat. 885, 50 U.S.C. (Appendix) 305 (g) (1940).

[43] The *Girouard* case was decided on the basis of statutory interpretation.

[44] Art. I, sec. 8, cl. 4.

[45] Terrace v. Thompson, 263 U.S. 197 (1923).

portation, Congress is omnicompetent. But while the Constitution does not confer upon aliens the right to naturalization, once Congress enacts a statute "there is a statutory right in the alien to submit his petition and evidence to a court, to have that tribunal pass upon them, and, if the requisite facts are established, to receive the certificate. . . . There is, of course, no 'right to naturalization unless all statutory requirements are complied with.' "[46]

POLITICAL OPINIONS

More and more, Congress has been including among the statutory requirements, which the petitioner for naturalization must satisfy, some that seriously touch upon the freedoms of speech, press, and assembly.

This trend began with the passing of an act in 1906,[47] which required the petitioner to state that "he is not a disbeliever in or opposed to organized government, or a member of or affiliated with an organization or body of persons teaching disbelief in or opposed to organized government, a polygamist or believer in the practice of polygamy." This act was intended to keep from anarchists and polygamists citizenship. Note should be taken, however, of its pattern: belief alone became a disqualification. It was not necessary for the government to prove that the petitioner had committed certain acts. Also, membership in or affiliation with an organization that teaches the proscribed doctrines became a disqualification. Also, the petitioner had to disavow doctrines and associations that were not proscribed for native-born citizens; thus, a distinction was made in the law between native-born and naturalized citizens with respect to enjoyment of certain fundamental freedoms.

This pattern has obtained ever since the enactment of

[46] Tutun v. U.S., 270 U.S. 568 (1926).
[47] 34 Stat. 596 (1906).

the 1906 statute and has been considerably extended and intensified. The most significant statutory enactments were adopted in 1940, 1950, and 1952. We shall examine these statutes briefly.

The Nationality Act of 1940[48] listed the classes of persons who may not be naturalized. The persons included in the prohibition are:

(1) Persons who believe in, advise, advocate or teach, or belong to or are affiliated with any organization, group, society, or association so advising, advocating, or teaching (a) opposition to all organized government; (b) the overthrow by force or violence of the Government of the United States or of all forms of law; (c) the duty, propriety, or necessity of unlawfully assaulting or killing an officer or officers of any organized government or of the United States Government because of their official character; (d) the unlawful damage, injury, or destruction of property; or (e) sabotage.

(2) Persons who write, publish, or cause to be written or published, or who knowingly circulate or cause to be circulated, distributed, printed, published, or displayed, or who knowingly possess for the foregoing purposes any written or printed matter advising, advocating, or teaching the doctrines enumerated above in (1).

(3) Persons who are members of or affiliated with any organization which does any of the acts specified in (2).[49]

The act also provides that giving, loaning, or promising of financial aid to be used for the advocacy or teaching of any doctrine proscribed in the statute shall constitute the advocacy or teaching of the doctrine and membership in or affiliation with an organization.

The provisions of the act are applicable to anyone who has been in the proscribed classes within a period of ten

[48] Sec. 305.
[49] *Op. cit. supra* note 22, pp. 716-717.

years preceding the filing of the naturalization petition, regardless of the fact that his activity may have ceased.

This act went beyond the 1906 act in these essential aspects: (1) It proscribes not only belief, but also advocacy and teaching; (2) it proscribes membership in or affiliation with organizations that advocate or teach the overthrow of the government of the United States by force or violence, as well as such personal advocacy or teaching; (3) it proscribes the publication of these doctrines, or the possession of printed matter with the purpose to publish these doctrines, or membership in or affiliation with an organization that publishes these doctrines, or the making of financial contributions toward the spreading of these doctrines; (4) it proscribes conduct, membership, or affiliation not only at the time of the filing of the petition for naturalization but at any time within ten years preceding such filing.

The intention of these prohibitions was to prevent Communists from acquiring citizenship through naturalization. The *Nationality Manual,*[50] attempting to implement the act, listed the Communist Party of the United States and the Socialist Workers Party of America[51] as coming within the proscription.[52] But the courts had before them an act of Congress that failed to mention organizations by name; they refused, therefore, to hold the Communist party a proscribed organization *eo nomine.*[53]

An attempt to reduce this difficulty was made by Congress in the Internal Security Act of 1950.[54] It made the fol-

[50] Sec. 754.

[51] A Trotskyite organization founded in 1937.

[52] The only other organizations listed in the *Nationality Manual*—The International Workers of the World (The IWW) and the Young Communist League—are unimportant; the former was moribund, the latter has been dissolved. *Op. cit. supra* note 22, p. 717.

[53] Schneiderman v. U.S., 320 U.S. 118 (1943); Bridges v. Wixon, 326 U.S. 135 (1945). See these cases discussed in Konvitz, *op. cit. supra* note 29, pp. 59-78, 119-136.

[54] Sec. 25, which amended sec. 305 of the Nationality Code of 1940.

lowing significant additions to the law: No person shall become naturalized if he is a member of or affiliated with any "Communist action organization" that is required to be registered under the terms of the Subversive Activities Control Act of 1950.[55] Proscribed advocacy was extended to include "the economic, international, and governmental doctrines of world communism or the economic or governmental doctrines of any other form of totalitarianism." The ten-year relation-back provision was continued, and there was added the provision that membership in or affiliation with a proscribed organization within five years *after* a person has been naturalized shall be "prima facie evidence that such person was not attached to the principles of the Constitution . . . at the time of naturalization."

While this amendment prevented Communists from acquiring naturalization easily, it left upon the government the burden of proving that the Communist party is in fact a "Communist action organization" required to register under the terms of the Subversive Activities Control Act of 1950. The compulsory registration procedures are, as President Truman pointed out in his message vetoing the measure,[56] time consuming.[57] However, once it was finally decided that the Communist party is subject to the registration provisions, proof of the character of the organization in each naturalization proceeding would not be necessary. From the point of view of Congress, the 1950 act was an improvement, but did not go far enough.

[55] The Subversive Activities Control Act of 1950 is Title I of the Internal Security Act of 1950.

[56] Message of September 22, 1950. Text in the *New York Times*, September 23, 1950.

[57] The Communist party was alleged to be subject to the registration requirements on November 22, 1950, in a petition of the Attorney General filed with the Subversive Activities Control Board. On April 20, 1953, the board ordered the party to register.

An attempt to eliminate (and not merely reduce) the difficulty was made in the Immigration and Nationality Act of 1952. This act made the following significant additions:[58] No person shall be naturalized "who is a member of or affiliated with . . . the Communist Party of the United States." There is no indirection, no circumlocution, no room for a judicial inquiry, no possibility of a defense denying guilt because of association.[59] The proscription falls also upon membership in or affiliation with "the direct predecessors or successors" of the Communist party, regardless of the name it may adopt. (This provision was written into the law to meet President Truman's criticism of the registration requirement in the 1950 act. He pointed out in his veto message that after it was finally held that the Communist party is required to register, the party might change its name, and then the procedures would need to be gone through once more against the "new" organization; and this cat-and-mouse game could go on indefinitely.) The act continues the ten-year relation-back[60] and the prospective five-year[61] provisions of the 1950 act.

There are additional provisions (mentioned in the preceding chapter) which further tend to differentiate the native-born and the naturalized citizen, especially the following: (1) If a naturalized person, within five years after naturalization, goes to a foreign country and takes permanent residence there, his certificate of naturalization may be set aside.[62] (2) Refusal on the part of a naturalized citizen, within ten years following his naturalization, to testify

[58] Sec. 313.

[59] Cf. opinion of Justice Murphy in the *Schneiderman* case, cited *supra* note 53.

[60] Sec. 313 (c). [61] Sec. 340 (c).

[62] Sec. 340 (d); similar to sec. 404 (c) of the 1940 act. See Lapides v. Clark, 176 F. 2 d 619.

as a witness before a congressional committee concerning his subversive activities, and his conviction of contempt for such refusal, may be ground for revocation of his naturalization.[63]

In drafting these provisions Congress obviously followed the recommendation of the Senate Committee on the Judiciary, which had reported in 1950: "Congress could provide that membership [in the Communist party] alone would bar naturalization. There seems to be no doubt whatever that, if membership in or affiliation with the [Communist] party, in itself, were made a statutory bar to naturalization, Congress would be acting entirely within its constitutional plenary power."[64]

The failure of the Supreme Court to find that the Communist party of the United States advocates or teaches the overthrow of the government by force or violence[65] led Congress to make this finding of fact. This has been done, in the 1952 statute, explicitly; nothing on this point is left to inference or to proof in accordance with the judicial rules of evidence. It is difficult to see how the court could upset or even controvert this legislative finding of fact.

The only line of argument available to the court, which might lead to the invalidation of the law, is that Congress prohibits aliens and naturalized citizens from enjoying freedoms and rights that are open to enjoyment by natural-

[63] Sec. 340 (a).

[64] *Op. cit. supra* note 22, pp. 719-720.

[65] In Dennis v. U.S., 341 U.S. 494 (1951), the court found the defendants guilty of violating section 3 of the Smith Act, 18 U.S.C. 2385 (1940) by conspiring to organize the Communist party as a group to teach and advocate the overthrow of the Government of the United States by force and violence. This was the first time the court went so far as to assimilate the Communist party to the class of organizations set up to teach and advocate the overthrow of the government by force and violence under a statute that does not name the party as a proscribed organization. But the decision has application only to co-conspirators, organizers of the party. Its usefulness by the government in a naturalization proceeding, in the absence of statutes adopted since the Smith Act, is open to doubt; this is why the 1952 act went all the way to eliminate doubt by explicitly naming the party.

born citizens, for the latter may be members of or affiliated with the Communist party without suffering loss of citizenship. Thus, with respect to the enjoyment of some fundamental freedoms, we have two classes of persons, and even two classes of citizens. But it is extremely doubtful if the Supreme Court will take this position. A decision of the court at the end of 1952 at least *sub silentio* affirmed the right of Congress to treat the native-born differently from the naturalized citizen;[66] nor is there any decision which throws doubt upon the proposition that the power of Congress to deal with naturalization is plenary. There are statements in some Supreme Court cases that imply a protest against the creation of a second-class citizenship. Mr Justice Douglas has said, e.g., that "Citizenship obtained through naturalization is not a second-class citizenship. . . . It is plain that citizenship attained through naturalization carries with it the privilege of full participation in the affairs of our society."[67] Similar statements have been made by Mr. Justice Rutledge,[68] and even by Chief Justice Marshall.[69] But decisions of the court made as recently as 1949[70] and 1952[71] show that the court has no intention to upset the will of Congress in its formulation of a uniform rule of naturalization. Perhaps, however, Congress will take to heart what General Eisenhower has said: "Only second-class Americanism tolerates second-class citizenship. It's time to get rid of both, and that includes rewriting the unfair provisions of the McCarran Immigration Act."[72]

[66] Mandoli v. Acheson, 73 S. Ct. 135 (1952).

[67] Knauer v. U.S., 328 U.S. 654 (1946).

[68] Schneiderman v. U.S., 320 U.S. 118 (1943).

[69] Osborn v. U.S. Bank, 9 Wheat. (U.S.) 738 (1824).

[70] Lapides v. Clark, 176 F. 2d 619 (1949); cert. den. 70 S. Ct. 101 (1949); rearg. den. 70 S. Ct. 187 (1949). The dissenting opinion of Judge Edgerton in the U.S. Court of Appeals (D.C. Circuit) is a notable one.

[71] Case cited *supra* note 66.

[72] Speech in Boston, October 21, 1952; *New York Times*, October 22, 1952.

WOMEN

The position of women with regard to naturalization ought to be briefly examined, for until recently they were denied equality of treatment with men. Prior to 1922 a woman automatically changed her citizenship by marriage: an alien woman acquired American citizenship by marriage to an American citizen, and an American woman lost her citizenship by marriage to an alien. A law of 1922 changed this. It provided "that the right of any woman to become a naturalized citizen of the United States shall not be denied or abridged because of her sex or because she is a married woman."[73]

This act provided that an alien woman could become an American citizen by naturalization only,[74] and that an American woman who married an alien shall maintain her American citizenship, unless she formally renounces it. This legislation followed the adoption of the Nineteenth Amendment to the Constitution in 1920, which provided that the right of citizens to vote shall not be denied or abridged on account of sex. The 1922 act "was regarded as a step in the general movement for the political emancipation of women."[75] On the other hand, it was contended that the act was "out of harmony with the essential principle of family unity and identity of interests of husband and wife."[76]

The Immigration and Nationality Act of 1952[77] continues the provision of the Nationality Code of 1940,[78] that the right of a person to become a naturalized citizen shall not be denied or abridged because of sex or because such person is married.[79]

[73] 42 Stat. 1021 (1922), known as the Cable Act. See L. Gettys, *The Law of Citizenship in the United States* (1934), ch. v.

[74] The process of naturalization was simplified for her if she married an American citizen. [75] Gettys, *op. cit.*, 141.

[76] *Ibid.* [77] Sec. 311. [78] 8 U.S.C. 702.

[79] An alien who marries an American citizen may become naturalized

While breaking up the legal fiction of the unity of husband and wife (with legal personality vested exclusively in the husband) may have, in some instances, the effect of lessening family unity and identity of interests, there can be no doubt that the equal naturalization and citizenship rights of men and women is a reaffirmation of "faith in fundamental human rights, in the dignity and worth of the human person."[80] Freedom and equality create problems, but freedom and equality also provide the will, intelligence and resources for the solution of these problems; for it is true, as the U.N. Commission on the Status of Women has said, that

> Well-being and progress of society depend on the extent to which both men and women are able to develop their personality and are cognizant of their responsibilities to themselves and to each other;
>
> Woman has thus a definite role to play in the building of a free, healthy, prosperous and moral society and she can fulfill this obligation only as a free and responsible member.[81]

CONCLUSION

American naturalization policy has been broadened over the years so that only relatively few persons find in the law insuperable difficulties. From 1907 to 1948 over 6,300,000 aliens have taken advantage of the naturalization laws.[82] The peak year was 1944, when 441,979 aliens were naturalized.[83] From 1798 to 1802 the length of residence as a prerequisite was fourteen years; since the latter year it has been five years.[84] As to literacy, the requirement of the Nationality Code of 1940 was that the petitioner was to prove

---

through simplified procedures. Sec. 319 of the Immigration and Nationality Act of 1952.

[80] Preamble to Charter of United Nations.

[81] Quoted in *These Rights and Freedoms,* U. N. Dept. of Information (1950), 112.

[82] *Op. cit. supra* note 22, p. 680. [83] *Ibid.* [84] *Ibid.,* 697.

his ability to speak the English language.[85] The requirement is less liberal under the 1952 act; now the petitioner must demonstrate "an understanding of the English language, including an ability to read, write, and speak words in ordinary usage in the English language."[86] The act provides, however, that this requirement shall be met "if the applicant can read or write simple words and phrases to the end that a reasonable test of his literacy shall be made and that no extraordinary or unreasonable condition shall be imposed upon the applicant."[87]

The 1940 act provided that the petitioner be a person of good moral character, attached to the principles of the Constitution, and well disposed to the good order and happiness of the United States.[88] The committing of offences from manslaughter or second-degree murder to bigamy or conducting a disorderly house have been held as negating good moral character.[89] That the test of "good moral character" is a variable one, which may lead to opposite findings, depending on what judge the alien petitioner is lucky or unlucky enough to face, is shown by a recent case[90] in which the Court of Appeals, with an opinion by Judge Learned Hand, held that a college teacher of foreign languages met the test of "good moral character" though he had admitted in his affidavit, "in a moment of what may have been unnecessary frankness," that now and then he had engaged in sexual intercourse with single women. The question, said Judge Hand, is not free from doubt, but he did not see how the court could get any help from outside; it would not be practicable "to conduct an inquiry as to what is the common conscience on the point"; the court was dealing here with an "impalpable standard," and had to resort to their own "conjecture."[91]

[85] 8 U.S.C. 704. [86] Sec. 312. [87] *Ibid.* [88] 8 U.S.C. 707.
[89] *Op. cit. supra* note 22, p. 700. [90] Schmidt v. U.S., 177 F. 2d 450 (1949).
[91] Cf. discussion of the term crimes involving "moral turpitude," in

The 1952 act continues the same requirement as to proof of good moral character and attachment to the principles of the Constitution.[92] It adds, however, a provision that could be used by unsympathetic judges to deny naturalization. The new law requires "a knowledge and understanding of the fundamentals of the history, and of the principles and form of the government, of the United States."[93] This, like the test of good moral character, opens the door to the judge's subjective standards. Some years from now, reviewing the cases brought to test the correctness of the judges' application of the requirement of good moral character and the requirement added by the 1952 act, we shall, in all probability, be able to say: "How many aliens have been denied citizenship who would not have been had some other judge heard their cases, and vice versa, we many only guess. That is not government by law."[94]

The privilege of naturalization has been broadened so that the distinctions of race, color, or sex no longer apply. There is a liberal provision regarding pacifists. The provision barring Communists and other subversive aliens from naturalization is hardly definite in its terms, for its full meaning and sweep must await conclusive decisions as to what are the "Communist-action" and the "Communist-front" organizations that are required to register under the provisions of the Subversive Activities Control Act of 1950; and the term "affiliated with" must wait for final (if that is possible) judicial interpretation.[95] It will take years for these questions to be cleared up; in the meantime, many aliens who would, without doubt, make loyal, and even distinguished, American citizens will find themselves reluctant to apply

Jordan v. DeGeorge, 341 U.S. 223 (1951), a deportation case.

[92] Sec. 316. [93] Sec. 312.

[94] Cf. language of Jackson, dis. op., in case cited *supra* note 91.

[95] Cf. Schneiderman v. U.S., 320 U.S. 118 (1943), discussed in Konvitz, *op. cit. supra* note 29, pp. 119-136.

for naturalization because of the risk that a particular judge might refuse to grant them the privilege of citizenship; and the stigma of a refusal exceeds that of simple alienage in the notoriety which follows and in opening up dramatically the possibility of deportation.

These problems are aggravated by the provision that an alien shall be ineligible for naturalization if he has been a member of or affiliated with a proscribed organization at any time within a ten year period preceding the filing of the petition for naturalization, "notwithstanding that at the time the petition is filed he may not be included within such classes [of persons ineligible because of membership or affiliation]."[96]

The reason for this provision is that Congress, when it passed the McCarran-Walter Act, believed that the Communist apparatus in the United States is controlled by aliens and foreign-born persons. The Senate Committee on the Judiciary stated in its report that "the Attorney General of the United States presented before the subcommittee an analysis conclusively establishing that the Communist organization, the Communist apparatus in the United States is overwhelmingly under the control of aliens and foreign-born persons."[97] A study by the Attorney General of 4,984 "of the more militant members of the Communist Party" as of 1947 showed that 2,202 or 44 per cent were either born in Russia or had at least one parent who was born in Russia or were married to persons of "Russian stock." An additional 614 persons, or 12.5 per cent of the 4,984 persons studied, were "either of stock from the countries adjacent to Russia (Poland, Finland, Rumania, Lithuania, Turkey, Latvia, and Estonia) or were married to persons of such stock."[98] Combining these figures, the Attorney General stated, "it will

[96] Sec. 313 (c). [97] *Op. cit. supra* note 22, p. 783. [98] *Ibid.*, 784.

be seen that 2,816 or 56.5 per cent of the 4,984 cases analyzed, were either of stock from Russia or the adjacent countries or were married to persons of such stock." An additional 1,739 persons, or 34.9 per cent, were "either of stock from other foreign countries or were married to stock from other foreign countries." Combining all these figures, the Attorney General—and the Senate Committee on the Judiciary—found that 91.4 per cent of the 4,984 subjects were "either of foreign stock or were married to persons of foreign stock. . . . In only 429, or 8.6 per cent of the 4,984 cases, were the subject and his parents, and, if married, the spouse and the spouse's parents, all born in the United States."[99] On the basis of this report and the testimony of former Communists, the Senate Committee on the Judiciary concluded that "It is a well-established fact that both the leadership and membership of the Communist Party is recruited overwhelmingly from alien ranks."

The difficulty with the figures cited by the Attorney General is that they do not isolate the aliens from persons of "foreign stock" (one parent or both parents born abroad). To add to persons of "foreign stock" persons "married to persons of foreign stock" is to make the Attorney General's figures practically useless for policy-making purposes.

According to the Federal Bureau of Investigation, the Communist Party of the United States had a membership in the fiscal year ending June 30, 1951, of 37,000.[100] The 1940 census showed 11,109,620 foreign-born persons in the United States; 3,189,080 were aliens and 7,177,960 were naturalized citizens. The number of persons classified as "foreign white stock," i.e., foreign-born persons and native

[99] *Ibid.* Cf. *Subversive and Illegal Aliens in the United States.* Progress Report. Senate Committee on the Judiciary, 82d Cong., 1st sess. (1951). Also same, Progress Report. No. 2 (1951).

[100] *New York Times,* June 25, 1952. In the previous fiscal year the membership was 51,785.

Americans of foreign or mixed parentage, was 34,576,718. It is against this latter figure that the figures of the Attorney General need to be viewed. When viewed in this light, it would seem that inferences of far-reaching scope affecting indirectly or directly some 35,000,000 persons are drawn from a class made up of 4,555 persons (91.4 per cent of 4,984 persons who were the subjects of the Attorney General's study). Even if a large percentage of the Attorney General's subjects were aliens, one would need to exercise extreme caution in drawing from the figure policy conclusions that would affect the naturalization privilege of over 3,000,000 persons.

All of this is said without intending to minimize the danger inherent in the existence of 37,000 Communist party members. Certainly protective measures commensurate with the danger need to be formulated and implemented. One may seriously question, however, the proposition that subjecting our aliens who seek naturalization to extraordinary threats, burdens, and dangers, is a reasonable, protective measure.

An argument in favor of the ten-year relation-back provision may be that the Communist party has, as a matter of party strategy, formally expelled alien members *en masse*, and by this action has destroyed any significance that discontinued membership might otherwise have as an indication of a change of heart by the individual.[101] The Director of the F.B.I. has cautioned that "thousands of ex-members who left the party of their own accord still feel themselves Communists," though no longer actual members.[102]

The party, always conspiratorial in character, has intensified its clandestine character as a result of the new anti-Com-

[101] See Harisiades v. Shaughnessy, 72 S. Ct. 512 (1952), opinion of Jackson, at p. 522.

[102] *Loc. cit. supra* note 100.

munist legislation and the disclosure in the Communist trials that government agents had infiltrated into the party and had learned many of its secrets. Thus the argument becomes circular: new laws and government strategy drive the party underground and lead to the formal (though not real) expulsion from the party of alien members; this in turn leads to more new laws thought to have become necessary by these developments.

The ten-year relation-back rule is too far-reaching a sword. It makes practically impossible an "escape by reformation."[103] Atonement and redemption ought to be made easier. Government agencies ought to be able to separate the genuine ex-Communists from the spurious ones; they do not need ten years to accomplish this end. On the contrary, the boon of citizenship, held out as a spiritual as well as a tangible inducement, might help considerably in our struggle against the Communist apparatus. We should use the instrumentality of charity no less than the instrumentalities of fear and punishment. "This only is charity," said John Donne, "to do all, all that we can." Charity can be a genuinely creative social force, William James has said; it can make real a degree of virtue which it alone assumes as possible.[104] Justices Douglas and Black have reminded us that we have no right to assume that a person who was once a Communist is tainted for all time and is forever dangerous to our society.[105] In this sentiment they echoed the statement of James that "We have no right to speak of human crocodiles and boa-constrictors as of fixedly incurable beings."[106] There are times, he said, when worldly wisdom or prudence needs to be transcended, when charity is to be trusted to

[103] Justice Jackson, case cited *supra* note 101.
[104] *The Varieties of Religious Experience* (1902).
[105] Dis. op. in case cited *supra* note 101, p. 523.
[106] *Op. cit. supra* note 104.

turn enemies into friends. Citizenship ought to be given with a hand that is held out in a spirit of free fellowship, welcoming the person, even—or perhaps especially—the ex-Communist, into a commonwealth that places a high value on brotherhood, love, and justice. "Brethren, if a man be overtaken in a fault, ye which are spiritual, restore such an one in the spirit of meekness."[107] For a nation of 160,000,000 persons, that has come out victorious in two world wars, to show fear in the face of aliens who admit to *former* membership in the Communist party, is to debase ourselves and to place too great a reliance on fear: "There is no fear in love."[108]

> He drew a circle that shut me out—
> Heretic, rebel, a thing to flout.
> But Love and I had the wit to win:
> We drew a circle that took him in.[109]

[107] Galatians 6:1. [108] 1 John 4:18.
[109] "Outwitted," from *Poems of Edwin Markham*, Selected and Arranged by Charles L. Wallis (1950); quoted with permission of Harper & Brothers, publishers, and Virgil Markham.

APPENDIX I

President Truman's Message on Veto of McCarran-Walter Bill

To the House of Representatives:

I return herewith, without my approval, H.R. 5678, the proposed Immigration and Nationality Act.

In outlining my objections to this bill, I want to make it clear that it contains certain provisions that meet with my approval. This is a long and complex piece of legislation. It has 164 separate sections, some with more than forty subdivisions. It presents a difficult problem of weighing the good against the bad, and arriving at a judgment on the whole.

H.R. 5678 is an omnibus bill which would revise and codify all of our laws relating to immigration, naturalization and nationality.

A general revision and modernization of these laws unquestionably is needed and long overdue, particularly with respect to immigration. But this bill would not provide us with an immigration policy adequate for the present world situation.

Indeed, the bill, taking all its provisions together, would be a step backward and not a step forward. In view of the crying need for reform in the field of immigration, I deeply regret that I am unable to approve H.R. 5678.

In recent years our immigration policy has become a matter of major national concern. Long dormant questions about the effect of our immigration laws now assume first-rate importance. What we do in the field of immigration and naturalization is vital to the continued growth and internal development of the United States—to the economic and social strength of our country—which is the core of the defense of the free world.

Our immigration policy is equally, if not more, important to the conduct of our foreign relations and to our responsibilities of moral leadership in the struggle for world peace.

In one respect this bill recognizes the great international significance of our immigration and naturalization policy, and takes a step to improve existing laws. All racial bars to naturalization would be removed, and at least some minimum immigration quota would be afforded to each of the free nations of Asia.

I have long urged that racial or national barriers to naturalization be abolished. This was one of the recommendations in my civil rights message to the Congress on Feb. 2, 1948. On Feb. 19, 1951, the House of Representatives unanimously passed a bill to carry it out.

But now this most desirable provision comes before me embedded in a mass of legislation which would perpetuate injustices of long standing against many other nations of the world, hamper the efforts we are making to rally the men of East and West alike to the cause of freedom, and intensify the repressive and inhumane aspects of our immigration procedures. The price is too high, and in good conscience I cannot agree to pay it.

I want all our residents of Japanese ancestry, and all our friends throughout the Far East, to understand this point clearly. I cannot take the step I would like to take, and strike down the bars that prejudice has erected against them, without, at the same time, establishing new discriminations against the peoples of Asia and approving harsh and repressive measures directed at all who seek a new life within our boundaries.

I am sure that with a little more time and a little more discussion in this country the public conscience and the good sense of the American people will assert themselves, and we shall be in a position to enact an immigration and naturalization policy that will be fair to all.

In addition to removing racial bars to naturalization, the bill would permit American women citizens to bring their alien husbands to this country as non-quota immigrants, and enable alien husbands of resident women aliens to come in under the quota in a preferred status. These provisions would be a step toward preserving the integrity of the family under our immigration laws, and are clearly desirable.

The bill would also relieve transportation companies of some of the unjustified burdens and penalties now imposed upon them. In particular, it would put an end to the archaic requirement that carriers pay the expenses of aliens detained at the port of entry, even though such aliens have arrived with proper travel documents.

But these few improvements are heavily outweighed by other provisions of the bill which retain existing defects in our laws, and add many undesirable new features.

The bill would continue, practically without change, the national origins quota system, which was enacted into law in 1924, and put into effect in 1929. This quota system—always based upon assumptions at variance with our American ideals—is long since out of date and more than ever unrealistic in the face of present world conditions.

This system hinders us in dealing with current immigration problems, and is a constant handicap in the conduct of our foreign relations. As I stated in my message to Congress on March 24, 1952, on the need for an emergency program of immigration from Europe:

"Our present quota system is not only inadequate to meet present emergency needs; it is also an obstacle to the development of an enlightened and satisfactory immigration policy for the long-run future."

The inadequacy of the present quota system has been demonstrated since the end of the war, when we were compelled to resort to emergency legislation to admit displaced persons. If the quota system remains unchanged, we shall be compelled to resort to similar emergency legislation again, in order to admit any substantial portion of the refugees from communism or the victims of overcrowding in Europe.

With the idea of quotas in general there is no quarrel. Some numerical limitation must be set, so that immigration will be within our capacity to absorb. But the overall limitation of numbers imposed by the national origins quota system is too small for our needs today, and the country-by-country limitations create a pattern that is insulting to large numbers of our finest citizens, irritating to our Allies abroad, and foreign to our purposes and ideals.

The over-all quota limitation, under the law of 1924, restricted annual immigration to approximately 150,000. This was about one-seventh of 1 per cent of our total population in 1920. Taking into account the growth in population since 1920, the law now allows us but one-tenth of 1 per cent of our total population. And since the largest national quotas are only partly used, the number actually coming has been in the neighborhood of one-fifteenth of 1 per cent.

This is far less than we must have in the years ahead to keep up with the growing needs of our Nation for manpower to maintain the strength and vigor of our economy.

The greatest vice of the present quota system, however, is that it discriminates, deliberately and intentionally, against many of the peoples of the world. The purpose behind it was to cut down and virtually eliminate immigration to this country from Southern and Eastern Europe.

A theory was invented to rationalize this objective. The theory was that in order to be readily assimilable, European immigrants should be admitted in proportion to the numbers of persons of their respective national stocks already here as shown by the census of 1920.

Since Americans of English, Irish and German descent were most numerous, immigrants of those three nationalities got the lion's share—more than two-thirds of the total quota. The re-

maining third was divided up among all the other nations given quotas.

The desired effect was obtained. Immigration from the newer sources of Southern and Eastern Europe was reduced to a trickle. The quotas allotted to England and Ireland remained largely unused, as was intended. Total quota immigration fell to a half or a third—and sometimes even less—of the annual limit of 154,000.

People from such countries as Greece, or Spain, or Latvia were virtually deprived of any opportunity to come here at all, simply because Greeks or Spaniards or Latvians had not come here before 1920 in any substantial numbers.

The idea behind this discriminatory policy was, to put it baldly, that Americans with English or Irish names were better people and better citizens than Americans with Italian or Greek or Polish names. It was thought that people of West European origin made better citizens than Rumanians or Yugoslavs or Ukranians or Hungarians or Balts or Austrians.

Such a concept is utterly unworthy of our traditions and our ideals. It violates the great political doctrine of the Declaration of Independence that "all men are created equal." It denies the humanitarian creed inscribed beneath the Statue of Liberty proclaiming to all nations:

"Give me your tired, your poor, your huddled masses yearning to breathe free."

It repudiates our basic religious concepts, our belief in the brotherhood of man, and in the words of St. Paul that "there is neither Jew nor Greek, there is neither bond nor free . . . for ye are all one in Christ Jesus."

The basis of this quota system was false and unworthy in 1924. It is even worse now. At the present time this quota system keeps out the very people we want to bring in. It is incredible to me that, in this year of 1952, we should again be enacting into law such a slur on the patriotism, the capacity and the decency of a large part of our citizenry.

Today we have entered into an alliance, the North Atlantic Treaty, with Italy, Greece and Turkey against one of the most terrible threats mankind has ever faced. We are asking them to join with us in protecting the peace of the world. We are helping them to build their defenses, and train their men, in the common cause. But through this bill we say to their people:

You are less worthy to come to this country than Englishmen or Irishmen; you Italians, who need to find homes abroad in the hundreds of thousands—you shall have a quota of 5,645; you Greeks, struggling to assist the helpless victims of a Communist civil war—you shall have a quota of 308; and you Turks, you are brave defenders of the Eastern flank, but you shall have a quota of only 225!

Today, we are "protecting" ourselves, as we were in 1924, against being flooded by immigrants from Eastern Europe. This is fantastic. The countries of Eastern Europe have fallen under the Communist yoke—they are silenced, fenced off by barbed wire and mine fields—no one passes their borders but at the risk of his life.

We do not need to be protected against immigrants from these countries—on the contrary we want to stretch out a helping hand, to save those who have managed to flee into Western Europe, to succor those who are brave enough to escape from barbarism, to welcome and restore them against the day when their countries will, as we hope, be free again.

But this we cannot do, as we would like to do, because the quota for Poland is only 6,500, as against the 138,000 exiled Poles, all over Europe, who are asking to come to these shores; because the quota for the now subjugated Baltic countries is little more than 700—against the 23,000 Baltic refugees imploring us to admit them to a new life here; because the quota for Rumania is only 289, and some 30,000 Rumanians, who have managed to escape the labor camps and the mass deportations of their Soviet masters, have asked our help. These are only a few examples of the absurdity, the cruelty of carrying over into this year of 1952 the isolationist limitations of our 1924 law.

In no other realm of our national life are we so hampered and stultified by the dead hand of the past as we are in this field of immigration. We do not limit our cities to their 1920 boundaries—we do not hold our corporations to their 1920 capitalizations—we welcome progress and change to meet changing conditions in every sphere of life, except in the field of immigration.

The time to shake off this dead weight of past mistakes is now. The time to develop a decent policy of immigration—a fitting instrument for our foreign policy and a true reflection of the ideals we stand for, at home and abroad—is now.

In my earlier message on immigration, I tried to explain to the Congress that the situation we face in immigration is an emergency—that it must be met promptly. I have pointed out that in the last few years, we have blazed a new trail in immigration, through our displaced-persons program.

Through the combined efforts of the Government and private agencies, working together not to keep people out, but to bring qualified people in, we summoned our resources of good will and human feeling to meet the task. In this program, we have found better techniques to meet the immigration problems of the 1950's.

None of this fruitful experience of the last three years is reflected in this bill before me. None of the crying human needs of this time of trouble is recognized in this bill. But it is not too late. The Congress can remedy these defects, and it can adopt legislation to meet the most critical problems before adjournment.

The only consequential change in the 1924 quota system which the bill would make is to extend a small quota to each of the countries of Asia. But most of the beneficial effects of this gesture are offset by other provisions of the bill. The countries of Asia are told in one breath that they shall have quotas for their nationals, and in the next, that the nationals of the other countries, if their ancestry is as much as 50 per cent Asian, shall be charged to these quotas.

It is only with respect to persons of Oriental ancestry that this invidious discrimination applies. All other persons are charged to the country of their birth. But persons with Asian ancestry are charged to the countries of Asia, wherever they may have been born, or however long their ancestors have made their homes outside the land of their origin. These provisions are without justification.

I now wish to turn to the other provisions of the bill, those dealing with the qualifications of aliens and immigrants for admission, with the administration of the laws, and with problems of naturalization and nationality. In these provisions, too, I find objections that preclude my signing this bill.

The bill would make it even more difficult to enter our country. Our resident aliens would be more easily separated from homes and families under grounds of deportation, both new and old, which would specifically be made retroactive. Admission to our citizenship would be made more difficult; expulsion from our citizenship would be made easier. Certain rights of native-born, first-generation Americans would be limited.

All our citizens returning from abroad would be subjected to serious risk of unreasonable invasions of privacy. Seldom has a bill exhibited the distrust evidenced here for citizens and aliens alike—at a time when we need unity at home, and the confidence of our friends abroad.

We have adequate and fair provisions in our present law to protect us against the entry of criminals. The changes made by the bill in those provisions would result in empowering minor immigration and consular officials to act as prosecutor, judge and jury in determining whether acts constituting a crime have been committed. Worse, we would be compelled to exclude certain people because they have been convicted by "courts" in Communist countries that know no justice.

Under this provision, no matter how construed, it would not be possible for us to admit many of the men and women who have stood up against totalitarian repression and have been punished for doing so. I do not approve of substituting totalitarian vengeance for democratic justice. I will not extend full faith and credit to the judgments of the Communist secret police.

The realities of a world only partly free would again be ignored in the provision flatly barring entry to those who made misrepresentations in securing visas. To save their lives and the lives of loved ones still imprisoned, refugees from tyranny sometimes misstate various details of their lives.

We do not want to encourage fraud. But we must recognize that conditions in some parts of the world drive our friends to desperate steps. An exception restricted to cases involving misstatement of country of birth is not sufficient. And to make refugees from oppression forever deportable on such technical grounds is shabby treatment indeed.

Some of the new grounds of deportation which the bill would provide are unnecessarily severe. Defects and mistakes in admission would serve to deport at any time because of the bill's elimination, retroactively as well as prospectively, of the present humane provision barring deportations on such grounds five years after entry.

Narcotic drug addicts would be deportable at any time, whether or not the addiction was culpable, and whether or not cured. The threat of deportation would drive the addict into hiding beyond the reach of cure, and the danger to the country from drug addiction would be increased.

I am asked to approve the reenactment of highly objectionable provisions now contained in the Internal Security Act of 1950—a measure passed over my veto shortly after the invasion of South Korea. Some of these provisions would empower the Attorney General to deport any alien who has engaged or has had a purpose to engage in activities "prejudicial to the public interest" or "subversive to the national security."

No standards or definitions are provided to guide discretion in the exercise of powers so sweeping. To punish undefined "activities" departs from traditional American insistence on established standards of guilt. To punish an undefined "purpose" is thought control.

These provisions are worse than the infamous Alien Act of 1798, passed in a time of national fear and distrust of foreigners, which gave the President power to deport any alien deemed "dangerous to the peace and safety of the United States." Alien residents were thoroughly frightened and citizens much disturbed by that threat to liberty.

Such powers are inconsistent with our democratic ideals. Conferring powers like that upon the Attorney General is unfair to him as well as to our alien residents. Once fully informed of such vast discretionary powers vested in the Attorney General, Americans now would and should be just as alarmed as Americans were in 1798 over less drastic powers vested in the President.

Heretofore, for the most part, deportation and exclusion have rested upon findings of fact made upon evidence. Under this bill, they would rest in many instances upon the "opinion" or "satisfaction" of immigration or consular employees. The change from objective findings to subjective feelings is not compatible with our system of justice. The result would be to restrict or eliminate judicial review of unlawful administrative action.

The bill would sharply restrict the present opportunity of citizens and alien residents to save family members from deportation. Under the procedures of present law, the Attorney General can exercise his discretion to suspend deportation in meritorious cases. In each such case, at the present time, the exercise of administrative discretion is subject to the scrutiny and approval of the Congress.

Nevertheless, the bill would prevent this discretion from being used in many cases where it is now available, and would narrow the circle of those who can obtain relief from the letter of the law. This is most unfortunate, because the bill, in its other provisions, would impose harsher restrictions and greatly increase the number of cases deserving equitable relief.

Native-born American citizens who are dual nationals would be subjected to loss of citizenship on grounds not applicable to other native-born American citizens. This distinction is a slap at millions of Americans whose fathers were of alien birth.

Children would be subjected to additional risk of loss of

citizenship. Naturalized citizens would be subjected to the risk of denaturalization by any procedure that can be found to be permitted under any state law or practice pertaining to minor civil-law suits.

Judicial review of administrative denials of citizenship would be severely limited and impeded in many cases, and completely eliminated in others. I believe these provisions raise serious constitutional questions. Constitutionality aside, I see no justification in national policy for their adoption.

Section 401 of this bill would establish a Joint Congressional Committee on Immigration and Nationality Policy. This committee would have the customary powers to hold hearings and to subpoena witnesses, books, papers and documents. But the committee would also be given powers over the executive branch which are unusual and of a highly questionable nature.

Specifically, Section 401 would provide that "the Secretary of State and the Attorney General shall without delay submit to the committee all regulations, instructions, and all other information as requested by the committee relative to the administration of this Act."

This section appears to be another attempt to require the executive branch to make available to Congress administrative documents, communications between the President and his subordinates, confidential files, and other records of that character. It also seems to imply that the committee would undertake to supervise or approve regulations. Such proposals are not consistent with the constitutional doctrine of the separation of powers.

In these and many other respects, the bill raises basic questions as to our fundamental immigration and naturalization policy, and the laws and practices for putting that policy into effect.

Many of the aspects of the bill which have been most widely criticized in the public debate are reaffirmations or elaborations of existing statutes or administrative procedures.

Time and again, examination discloses that the revisions of existing law that would be made by the bill are intended to solidify some restrictive practice of our immigration authorities, or to overrule or modify some ameliorative decision of the Supreme Court or other Federal courts.

By and large, the changes that would be made by the bill do not depart from the basically restrictive spirit of our existing laws—but intensify and reinforce it.

These conclusions point to an underlying condition which deserves the most careful study. Should we not undertake a reassessment of our immigration policies and practices in the light of the conditions that face us in the second half of the twentieth century?

The great popular interest which this bill has created, and the criticism which it has stirred up, demand an affirmative answer. I hope the Congress will agree to a careful re-examination of this entire matter.

To assist in this complex task, I suggest the creation of a representative commission of outstanding Americans to examine the basic assumptions of our immigration policy, the quota system and all that goes with it, the effect of our present immigration and nationality laws, their administration, and the ways in which they can be brought into line with our national ideals and our foreign policy.

Such a commission should, I believe, be established by the Congress. Its membership should be bipartisan and divided equally among persons from private life and persons from public life. I suggest that four members be appointed by the President, four by the President of the Senate, and four by the Speaker of the House of Representatives.

The commission should be given sufficient funds to employ a staff and it should have adequate powers to hold hearings, take testimony, and obtain information. It should make a report to the President and to the Congress within a year from the time of its creation.

Pending the completion of studies by such a commission, and the consideration of its recommendations by the Congress, there are certain steps which I believe it is most important for the Congress to take this year.

First, I urge the Congress to enact legislation removing racial barriers against Asians from our laws. Failure to take this step profits us nothing and can only have serious consequences for our relations with the peoples of the Far East. A major contribution to this end would be the prompt enactment by the Senate of H.R. 403. That bill, already passed by the House of Representatives, would remove the racial bars to the naturalization of Asians.

Second, I strongly urge the Congress to enact the temporary emergency immigration legislation which I recommended three months ago. In my message of March 24, 1952, I advised the Congress that one of the gravest problems arising from the present world crisis is created by the overpopulation in parts of Western Europe. That condition is aggravated by the flight and expulsion of people from behind the Iron Curtain.

In view of these serious problems, I asked the Congress to authorize the admission of 300,000 additional immigrants to the United States over a three-year period. These immigrants would include Greek nationals, Dutch nationals, Italians from Italy and Trieste, Germans and persons of German ethnic origin, and religious and political refugees from communism in Eastern Europe.

This temporary program is urgently needed. It is very important that the Congress act upon it this year. I urge the Congress to give prompt and favorable consideration to the bills introduced by Senator Hendrickson and Representative Celler (S. 3109 and H.R. 7376), which will implement the recommendations contained in my message of March 24.

I very much hope that the Congress will take early action on these recommendations. Legislation to carry them out will correct some of the unjust provisions of our laws, will strengthen us at home and abroad, and will serve to relieve a great deal of the suffering and tension existing in the world today.

HARRY S. TRUMAN

The White House
June 25, 1952

APPENDIX II

President Truman's Messages on Aid to Refugees and Displaced Persons

I

It is with very great reluctance that I have signed S. 2242, the Displaced Persons Act of 1948.

If the Congress were still in session, I would return this bill without my approval and urge that a fairer, more humane bill be passed. In its present form this bill is flagrantly discriminatory. It mocks the American tradition of fair play. Unfortunately, it was not passed until the last day of the session. If I refused to sign this bill now, there would be no legislation on behalf of displaced persons until the next session of the Congress.

It is a close question whether this bill is better or worse than no bill at all. After careful consideration I have decided, however, that it would not be right to penalize the beneficiaries of this bill on account of the injustices perpetrated against others who should have been included within its provisions. I have therefore signed the bill in the hope that its injustices will be rectified by the Congress at the first opportunity.

Americans of all religious faiths and political beliefs will find it hard to understand, as I do, why the Eightieth Congress delayed action on this subject until the end of this session, with the result that most attempts to improve the bill were frustrated.

The Eightieth Congress certainly had ample time to produce a satisfactory bill. Eighteen months ago, in my state of the Union message, I stated that I did not feel that the United States had done its part in the admission of displaced persons. I pointed out that Congressional assistance in the form of new legislation was needed.

Six months later, on July 7, 1947, because the Congress had not yet acted, I sent a special message on the subject. I reminded the Congress: "We are dealing with a human problem, a world tragedy. I urge the Congress to press forward with its consideration of this subject and to pass suitable legislation as speedily as possible."

To my regret, the Congress adjourned last summer without passing any displaced persons legislation.

Again, on Jan. 7, 1948, I urged the Congress "to pass suitable legislation at once so that this nation may do its share in caring for homeless and suffering refugees of all faiths. I believe that the admission of these persons will add to the strength and energy of the nation."

The Congress did not act "at once." The Senate committee charged with the responsibility of rendering a report on Jan. 10, 1948, asked for, and received, an extension to report on Feb. 10. Instead of reporting on Feb. 10 it reported on March 2.

The bill which it finally reported without a single public hearing, was roundly and deservedly criticized by all who were interested in achieving a fair solution of this problem. Through one device or another, debate on the bill by the Senate was postponed from the beginning of March until the end of May.

The Senate bill was not passed until June 2. The House of Representatives in the meantime had delayed action and did not pass its bill until June 11. It was not until the last days of the session that the Senate and the House conferees met to put together a compromise.

The compromise resulting from this hasty, last-minute action consisted largely of combining the worst features of both the Senate and House bills.

I have analyzed closely the bill which was sent to me for signature. Its good points can be stated all too briefly: at long last, the principle is recognized that displaced persons should be admitted to the United States. Two hundred thousand displaced persons may be admitted in the next two years, as well as 2,000 recent Czech refugees and 3,000 orphans.

The bad points of the bill are numerous. Together they form a pattern of discrimination and intolerance wholly inconsistent with the American sense of justice.

The bill discriminates in callous fashion against displaced persons of the Jewish faith. This brutal fact cannot be obscured by the maze of technicalities in the bill or by the protestations of some of its sponsors.

The primary device used to discriminate against Jewish displaced persons is the provision restricting eligibility to those displaced persons who entered Germany, Austria, or Italy on or before Dec. 22, 1945. Most of the Jewish displaced persons who had entered Germany, Austria, or Italy by that time have already left; and most of the Jewish displaced persons now in those areas arrived there after Dec. 22, 1945, and hence are denied a chance to come to the United States under this bill.

By this device more than 90 per cent of the remaining Jewish displaced persons are definitely excluded. Even the eligible 10 per cent are beset by numerous additional restrictions written into the bill.

For all practical purposes, it must be frankly recognized, therefore, that this bill excludes Jewish displaced persons, rather than accepting a fair proportion of them along with other faiths.

The bill also excludes many displaced persons of the Catholic faith who deserve admission. Many anti-Communist refugees of Catholic faith fled into the American zones after Dec. 22, 1945, in order to escape persecution in countries dominated by a Communist form of government. These, too, are barred by the Dec. 22, 1945, dateline.

It is inexplicable, except upon the abhorrent ground of intolerance, that this date should have been chosen instead of April 21, 1947, the date on which General Clay closed the displaced persons camps to further admissions.

The Jewish and Catholic displaced persons who found asylum in our zones between Dec. 22, 1945, and April 21, 1947, who are wrongly excluded by this bill, fled to their native countries for the same basic reasons as Balts who came before Dec. 22, 1945, and Czechs who came after January, 1948, who are rightly included. I sincerely hope that the Congress will remedy this gross discrimination at its earliest opportunity.

There are many other seriously objectionable features in the bill. Some of these are as follows:

Except for orphans, the bill charges the displaced persons admitted under its provisions to future immigration quotas of their countries of birth, up to 50 per cent of the quota per year. Under this system, 50 per cent of some quotas will be "mortgaged" for generations.

This is a most begruding method of accepting useful and worthy people and will necessarily deprive many other worthy people of an opportunity to come to the United States in future years. Considering how few permanent immigrants were able to enter this country during the war, it would have been more equitable to admit the displaced persons as non-quota immigrants.

The bill requires that at least 40 per cent of the displaced persons allowed to enter this country must come from areas which have been "de facto annexed by a foreign power." This guarantees a disproportionately high percentage of persons from particular areas.

It would have been fairer to provide instead for the admission of persons in proportion to the numbers of each group in the displaced persons camps.

The bill reflects a singular lack of confidence by the Congress in the capacity and willingness of the people of the United States to extend a welcoming hand to the prospective immigrants.

It contains many restrictive requirements, such as prior assurances of suitable employment and "safe and sanitary housing," unnecessarily complicated investigation of each applicant, and burdensome reports from individual immigrants. I regret that the Congress saw fit to impose such niggardly conditions.

The bill submitted to me also emasculates the salutary provision of the House bill which provided for the granting of permanent residence status to a maximum of 15,000 displaced persons who are already lawfully in this country. The bill now requires a concurrent resolution of the Congress in favor of each individual after his application has been approved by the Attorney General.

This requirement has the effect of perpetuating the cumbersome practice of special action by the Congress to adjust the status of individual aliens.

I know what a bitter disappointment this bill is—to the many displaced victims of persecution who looked to the United States for hope; to the millions of our citizens who wanted to help them in the finest American spirit; to the many members of the Congress who fought hard but unsuccessfully for a decent displaced persons bill. I hope that this bitter disappointment will not turn to despair.

I have signed this bill, in spite of its many defects, in order not to delay further the beginning of a resettlement program and in the expectation that the necessary remedial action will follow when Congress reconvenes.

HARRY S. TRUMAN

The White House
June 25, 1948

II

One of the gravest problems arising from the present world crisis is created by the overpopulation in parts of Western Europe, aggravated by the flight and expulsion of people from the oppressed countries of Eastern Europe.

This problem is of great practical importance to us because it affects the peace and security of the free world. It is also of great concern to us, because of our long-established humanitarian traditions. The Congress has recognized the importance of this problem and has already enacted some legislation to help meet it.

I ask the Congress to give early and favorable consideration to additional legislation to make more adequate provision for meeting this situation.

Specifically, I ask the Congress to authorize a program that will:

1. Provide aid for the unfortunate victims of oppression who are escaping from Communist tyranny behind the Iron Curtain,
2. Continue our participation in the international effort now being made to assist in the migration and resettlement throughout the world of a substantial number of persons from the overpopulated areas of Western Europe, and
3. Authorize additional immigration into this country, on a limited basis, to aid in alleviating the problems created by Communist tyrrany and overpopulation in Western Europe.

The solution to these problems cannot, and should not, be the responsibility of any one nation.

It is an international responsibility—an integral part of the world crisis which the free nations must meet together. It demands the cooperative efforts of all interested countries. But a real solution can be found only if the United States does its part. We have done our part in the past—we must not falter now.

World War II left in its wake a tremendous upheaval of populations in the countries of Europe. To meet the situation, this country took the lead in establishing the International Refugee Organization, which provided care and protection for displaced persons and made possible the migration of more than 1,000,000 of them to forty-eight countries throughout the free world.

As our own contribution to the common effort, the Congress in 1948 enacted the Displaced Persons Act and subsequently amended and extended it. Both the Congress and the American people have every right to be proud of the achievements made under this far-sighted humanitarian legislation.

The Displaced Persons Act is now approaching the termination date fixed by the Congress. When operations under this law have been finished, almost 400,000 victims of tyranny will have been resettled in the United States. The first major phase of the program was completed with the issuance of practically all of the 341,000 visas authorized to be issued by midnight, Dec. 31, 1951.

In addition, the Congress authorized the admission of 54,744 Germans who had fled or been driven from areas east of the Iron Curtain. There is every likelihood that the remaining visas for these German expellees will be issued ahead of the June 30, 1952 deadline set by the Congress.

The job has been well done by the Displaced Persons Commission and other cooperating agencies of the Government. Much of the success of the program is due to the vital work accomplished by private voluntary agencies, representing our major religious faiths and nationality groups, and by the state commissions appointed by the Governors of thirty-four states.

These organizations of citizens have contributed their efforts and resources to resettling the greater part of the displaced persons admitted to this country. Without them, and without the goodwill and cooperative response of thousands of American families and church groups, this great program could never have been carried out.

Thus, by doing our own share and by acting together with the other countries of the free world, we have been dealing successfully with the major dislocations caused by Hitler's policies of brutality and aggression.

But the movement of large masses of distressed people across international boundaries is by no means over. Communist tyranny has taken up where Hitler's brutality left off. We are, therefore, now turning our attention to the innocent and unhappy victims of Communist oppression.

Throughout the Soviet-dominated area of Central and Eastern Europe, the Communist regimes are increasing their repressive measures. Some of the enslaved people are managing to escape to the West. Some fifteen to twenty thousand Germans are slipping over the border from the Soviet zone of Germany and crossing into Western Germany every month.

From the Communist countries to the south and east the movement to free Europe is much smaller, but still they come, at the risk of their lives, past border guards and through mine fields. There are about 18,000 of these people already west of the Iron Curtain, and they are coming in at the rate of about 1,000 a month.

The people in all these groups come into areas where, for the most part, the local economy is unable to support the population already there.

Western Germany, for example, is overcrowded with almost 9,000,000 people of German ethnic origin who were driven there from Eastern Europe after the war.

Trieste, which is receiving many of those escaping from the satellites, is badly overcrowded.

Italy is struggling with very serious problems of overpopulation and is urgently trying to resettle large numbers of its people overseas.

Greece faces great difficulty in absorbing the refugees of Greek origin who are being driven out of the Balkan satellites by the Communists.

Thus, the brutal policies of Soviet tyranny are aggravating overcrowded conditions which are already a danger to the stability of these free nations.

This in general terms, is the nature of the problem that now confronts free Europe.

The Congress is aware of the importance of this problem for the free world and the security of the United States. Congressional enactments and appropriations recently enabled the United States to take the lead in establishing the provisional inter-governmental committee for the movement of migrants from Europe, which seventeen governments have already joined.

This organization is already at work providing overseas transportation for migrants from areas of overpopulation to lands where more people are needed.

We are taking part in the work of this organization and have contributed $10,000,000 to its operation. The organization has taken over the fleet of ships formerly operated by the International Refugee Organization.

The legal authority to participate in this organization is contained in the Mutual Security Act of 1951. This authority should be extended, and the Congress should make provision for continuing our financial contribution to this work for the next fiscal year.

This is of great importance, but much more needs to be done.

In the first place, specific aid and assistance should be provided for the people who are fleeing at the risk of their lives from Southern and Eastern Europe. These people are Balts, Poles, Czechs, Slovaks, Hungarians, Bulgarians, Rumanians, Albanians, Ukrainians and Russians.

These people face a desperate situation. Not only do they arrive destitute, with only what they can carry on their backs, but they find themselves in totally strange lands among strange peoples speaking strange languages.

The local authorities do not have adequate resources to care for them properly. These people need better care when they first arrive and they need assistance if they are to move on and resettle elsewhere.

The miserable conditions in which these fugitives from communism find themselves, and their present inability to emigrate to new homes and start new lives, lead inevitably to despair. Their disillusionment is being effectively exploited by Communist propaganda.

These men and women are friends of freedom. They include able and courageous fighters against communism. They ask only for an opportunity to play a useful role in the fight for freedom. It is the responsibility of the free world to afford them this opportunity.

The need is well recognized, both in Europe and in this country. Private welfare organizations of American citizens, Protestant, Catholic and Jewish, have been working hard to help these people. Last year, these organizations spent substantial amounts for their care and resettlement. These organizations will continue their efforts this year. But the need is greater than they can handle.

First of all, these fugitives from communism need supplemental care and maintenance after they arrive in Western Europe. Local governments and private relief organizations give a minimum of this type of aid, but their resources are inadequate. Additional food, better shelter, clothing, medical care, legal advice and other kinds of material assistance are needed.

These people also need assistance in financing overseas transportation. The new international migration organization and the American private relief agencies can and do help with this, but a concerted effort is needed to give these people an equal opportunity to share in the migration program.

At present, because of inadequate resources, it is these fugitives from communism who have the greatest difficulty in arranging for overseas migration. If funds were provided, and an adequate administrative organization set up, these people would have a better chance to migrate.

I am convinced that we must help these people. Therefore, acting under the authority of the Mutual Security Act of 1951, I am authorizing the Director for Mutual Security to go forward with a limited program of assistance in this fiscal year. Four million three hundred thousand dollars will be allocated for this purpose.

This program will help alleviate the condition of these people in the countries to which they escape and will enable many of them to move out of Europe. The funds that are being made available will supplement—but not in any sense supersede—the efforts now being made both by the governments of the countries where these people have sought refuge and by private American organizations.

Supplemental care and overseas migration do not, however, constitute all that should be done for those who escape from Eastern Europe. A substantial number of them want to stay in

Europe and should have the chance to do so. They should be welcomed in Western Europe and given the opportunity to make their individual contributions to the free world. Many of them will need further education or training so they can prepare themselves for useful and productive work in the North Atlantic community.

I urge the Congress, therefore, to provide clear and adequate authority for the coming fiscal year—together with the necessary funds—so that the program of assistance we are now starting for the refugees from communism can be carried forward and strengthened along the lines that I have mentioned here.

In addition to these types of aid, the opportunity for military service may provide an answer to the problems of a small number of these refugees. Some of these people will be able to enlist in the United States armed forces overseas, under Public Law 597, the so-called Lodge Act of 1950.

So far, however, only a handful have been allowed to do this. Security screening requirements have necessarily been high, since each person under the provisions of the Lodge Act is a potential United States citizen.

Another type of military service for these people is authorized under Section 101 (A) (q) of the Mutual Security Act of 1951, which provides that they can be formed into elements of the military forces supporting the North Atlantic Treaty Organization. The question of forming such units presents great administrative and political difficulties, but it has been receiving careful study.

Even if it proves possible, however, to create such units, military service could utilize only a relatively small number of these people, and would not eliminate the need for additional measures to use their skills and energies in civilian life.

Such, in brief, are the measures that can help to alleviate the problems of these fugitives from Soviet terror. But these problems, important as they are, are overshadowed by the need for increasing migration from the overcrowded areas of Europe.

Overpopulation is one of the major factors preventing the

fullest recovery of those countries where it exists. It is a serious drag on the economies of nations belonging to the North Atlantic Treaty Organization. A solution to this problem, therefore, becomes vitally necessary to strengthen the defense of the North Atlantic community.

Our common defense requires that we make the best possible use not only of the material resources of the free world but of our human resources as well. Men and women who cannot be productively employed in the free countries of Europe because of conditions there are a net loss to the strength of the free world.

In other countries, where they are needed, these same people could add to the output and growing power of the free nations. But left in idleness as they now are, wasted and hopeless, they become an easy prey to the demagogues of totalitarianism, both Right and Left.

The bulk of the emigration needed will have to be taken care of by countries other than the United States. Some of the free nations, particularly those with large unsettled areas or undeveloped resources, have a pressing need for large numbers of immigrants to build up their countries and increase their production.

Canada and Australia for example, have already initiated substantial programs of immigration. The Australian immigration program calls for an annual immigration of at least 150,000 persons per year. Canadian absorption in the last year was at the rate of 180,000. Additional opportunities for migrants are opening up, although more slowly, in the Republics of Central and South America.

But the United States can and should take some of the migrants now available in Europe. One of the reasons we lead the free world today is that we are a nation of immigrants. We have been made strong and vigorous by diverse skills and abilities of the different peoples who have migrated to this country and become American citizens. Past immigration has helped to build our tremendous industrial power. Today, our growing economy can make effective use of additional manpower in various areas and lines of work.

The rapid expansion of our industry and the enlargement of our defense forces, have increased the demands of our available manpower reserves. Our industry can readily absorb a limited number of skilled and trained personnel in the years immediately ahead.

In our agriculture particularly, we have a need for additional people. Farm operators and farm workers are essential in our defense effort. Since 1949, there has again been a downward trend in the farm population of the United States. With the resumption of the movement from the farms to the cities, there is a real danger that in the years just ahead our agricultural production may be seriously hampered.

A rich pool of surplus farmers and farm workers exists in the overpopulated areas of Western Europe. Among the expellees in Western Germany there are many agricultural families with no opportunity for employment on the land. In Italy and the Netherlands, too, there are large groups of agricultural workers who cannot find productive employment on the limited arable land available.

Besides farm workers, our experience under the Displaced Persons Act has demonstrated that we can obtain from Europe some trained factory workers, engineers, scientific technicians, and other kinds of specially qualified people whose skills can be put to good use in our economy.

I am convinced that we should welcome to this country a number of those who now must emigrate from Europe. We should do this, not only in our own self-interest, but also as a way to reaffirm the great tradition of freedom and opportunity which we have proved in our own experience to be the surest path of progress and prosperity.

In considering the steps to be taken, we should measure the needs of the distressed people in Europe against our own capacity to make good use of additional manpower, and the extent of our international responsibilities.

APPENDIX II

The problem we face is in the nature of an emergency. This emergency can be of limited duration, if we of the free world act wisely and resolutely. The plight of the refugees in Europe and the demands of our national defense are both related to the threat of Communist aggression. When that threat wanes, there will be less need for extraordinary measures. But while it persists, we should move promptly and effectively to meet it.

The existing immigration laws are inadequate—both in general and as regards this special problem. The Displaced Persons Act will end this year, and we will be thrown back on the quota system of immigration.

So far as the people escaping from communism are concerned, many of them will be completely blocked from coming to this country because their quotas have been "mortgaged" under the Displaced Persons Act, for many years in the future.

For example, half of the Latvian quota has been mortgaged ahead three centuries to the year 2274, the Estonian quota through the year 2146, the Lithuanian quota through the year 2087, and the Polish quota through the year 2000.

Furthermore, under present law we will be unable to make any substantial contribution to meeting the problem of overpopulation in Germany, the Netherlands, Italy or Greece. In the latter countries, for example, where the need is particularly acute, we can admit annually only 5,677 Italians and 310 Greeks under the law as it now stands.

To meet the present emergency, we should enlarge the numbers of immigrants that can be taken in from all these critical areas. I ask the Congress to authorize the admission of some 300,000 additional persons over a three-year period. This would include, on an annual basis:

1. 7,000 religious and political refugees from communism in Eastern Europe;
2. 7,500 Greek nationals form Greece;
3. 7,500 Dutch from the Netherlands;
4. 39,000 Italians from Italy and Trieste; and
5. 39,000 Germans and persons of German ethnic origin.

Immigration in these amounts and from these sources could readily be absorbed to this country, and, together with a far larger volume of immigration to other free countries, would go a long way toward solving the emergency problem in Europe.

While the admission of these particular groups should constitute a temporary program of limited duration, it could well be fitted into desirable permanent changes in our present immigration quota system if the Congress finds itself able to make such changes at this session.

Our present quota system is not only inadequate to meet present emergency needs, it is also an obstacle to the development of an enlightened and satisfactory immigration policy for the long-run future.

If our quotas were revised and made more flexible, they could probably be utilized to take care of most or all of the immigration required to meet the present emergency situation. The balance, if any, could be admitted without reference to quota numbers. These are considerations that the Congress will wish to keep in mind when it takes up the question of improving our over-all immigration laws.

It is most important to remember, however, that action to meet the emergency problem is needed this year. If the Congress cannot agree at this session on desirable improvements in our whole system of immigration that would take care of the emergency problem, it should act to take care of the emergency directly.

In no event should this vital emergency program be tied to or associated with restrictive changes in our permanent immigration laws—changes which would in themselves hamper or nullify the operation of the emergency program.

In addition to this emergency three-year program, I recommend that steps be taken to alleviate an unfortunate situation arising under the operation of the Displaced Persons Act.

Although all visas authorized for displaced persons were issued, some 7,500 of them were lost because the persons to whom they were issued did not actually come to the United States. On the other hand, a number of persons who were seeking admission under the act, and whose applications were under consideration, were unable to obtain visas prior to the time the authority to issue such visas expired on Dec. 31, 1951.

A substantial portion of these applicants were admissable under the standards of the act, and would have made as good immigrants as those already admitted. The voluntary agencies or individual citizens have given the assurances necessary for the admission of these persons. There is still place for them in the United States.

It seems unjust and unwise to deprive them of the opportunity for which they are qualified. Seven thousand five hundred visas should be ample to take care of the displaced persons in this category. I recommend that Congress authorize up to that number of visas for them.

In carrying out this proposal, and the three-year emergency program as well, we should follow the lessons of the successful experience we have had under the Displaced Persons Act.

The same kind of provision should be made, for example, for security safeguards with respect to those admitted to this country, for means to effect their settlement here on a wide geographic basis, and for safeguards against displacement of United States citizens from housing or employment. And similarly, as under the Displaced Persons Act, there should be no religious, racial or other discrimination in the selection of the immigrants.

With respect to the financing of the emergency three-year program, however, the situation is rather different from that under the Displaced Persons Act, where transportation was financed through Government funds.

Except for the refugees from communism, the people from the overpopulated areas, who constitute the bulk of the migrants to be admitted, are in a better financial position than the displaced persons of former years.

They are not stateless, or dependent wholly on charity. Their countries are interested in seeing them migrate and can be called on to help with the expense of getting them started. The migrants themselves can be asked to repay the cost of their overseas transportation, once they have resettled. Some of them have assets of their own which can be used.

While it may be advisable to provide a source of funds to be loaned to these migrants to pay for their passage, the net additional cost to this Government of transporting the people from the overpopulated areas should be small.

The years through which we are passing are tragic years for many people. We are faced with extraordinary problems which demand extraordinary solutions. The problem of the refugees from Communist tyranny and that of overpopulation in Western Europe are matters of practical concern to the entire free world.

To us in America, whose most basic belief is in the inherent worth of the human individual, these problems present a challenge as well as a responsibility.

The programs I have here recommended are designed to meet the challenge and accept the responsibility. I hope that the Congress will give them prompt and favorable consideration.

HARRY S. TRUMAN

The White House
March 24, 1952

APPENDIX III

President Eisenhower's Statements on Immigration

From State of Union Message, February 2, 1953

There is one sphere in which civil rights are inevitably involved in Federal legislation. This is the sphere of immigration.

It is a manifest right of our Government to limit the number of immigrants our nation can absorb. It is also a manifest right of our Government to set reasonable requirements on the character and the numbers of people who come to share our land and our freedom.

It is well for us, however, to remind ourselves occasionally of an equally manifest fact: we are—one and all—immigrants or the sons and daughters of immigrants.

Existing legislation contains injustices. It does, in fact, discriminate. I am informed by members of the Congress that it was realized, at the time of its enactment, that future study of the proper basis of determining quotas would be necessary.

I am therefore requesting the Congress to review this legislation and to enact a statute which will at one and the same time guard our legitimate national interest and be faithful to our basic ideas of freedom and fairness to all.

Letter to Senator Arthur V. Watkins:

Thank you for your letter of March 20 informing me of the plan of your subcommittee to hold hearings on several immigration bills now pending before it. I am particularly grateful to have your assurance that you are prepared to cooperate in the formulation and implementation of an immigration program, insofar as you can consistently do so.

It is only proper to point out to you that I have received a great many complaints that the Immigration and Nationality Act of 1952 does embody many serious and inequitable restrictions.

While I recognize that the act contains some provisions which represent a liberalizing influence in the field of immigration law and that a fundamental revision of a statute cannot be approached without searching analysis, I suggest that a study of the operation of many of the administrative provisions of the Immigration and Nationality Act of 1952 should be immediately undertaken, with an invitation to all concerned to testify regarding the provisions of which they complain.

In the State of the Union Message I pointed out that "existing legislation contains injustices." Among the administrative provisions of the law which it is claimed may operate with unwarranted harshness are the following:

1

The provisions which make inadmissible any alien who, in the opinion of the consul, is likely to become a public charge at any time in the future. This places upon the consul the burden of forecasting events which cannot be predicted and, it is claimed, would permit abuse of discretionary judgment.

2

The provisions which make ineligible for a visa any alien with respect to whom the consular officer knows or has reasonable ground to believe probably would, after entry, engage in espionage, sabotage or "subversive" activities. It is asserted that this provision vests in the consul the authority, without restraint, to determine by his own mental processes the probability of future proscribed conduct, thus permitting a possible abuse of discretionary judgment.

3

The provision which permits an immigration official to interrogate without warrant "any alien or person believed to be an alien as to his right to be or to remain in the United States." It is said that unless the word "believed" is clarified so as specifically to require "probable cause," an abuse of this authority could possibly subject any citizen to improper interrogation.

4

The provisions under which, it is asserted, naturalized citizens have only "second class" citizenship because they, as distinguished from native-born citizens, can be expatriated because of residence abroad for certain periods of time, without reference to any other conduct on their part.

5

New restriction upon granting leave to seamen while ships are in United States ports.

6

The provision which exempts from the criminal grounds of exclusion those aliens who have been convicted abroad of purely political offenses fails to define the term "political." It is asserted that it is therefore difficult for administrative officers to determine whether the "criminal" offenses for which individuals have been convicted are indeed of a criminal, as distinguished from a political, nature.

7

The provisions permitting aliens who were and are believers in nazism and fascism to enter the United States unless it can be affirmatively shown that they advocated the establishment of those ideologies in the United States.

8

Deportation provisions that permit an alien to be deported at any time after entry, irrespective of how long ago he was involved, after entry, in an activity or affiliation designated as "subversive." Such alien is now subject to deportation even if his prior affiliation was terminated many years ago and he has since conducted himself as a model American.

9

The provision which authorizes the Attorney General to suspend deportation of certain deportable aliens if "exceptional and extremely unusual hardship" is demonstrated. It is asserted, however, that these restrictive terms are not explained in the law, thus leaving the interpretation of the phrase open to administrative determination, subject to Congressional approval or "veto." It is argued that the law should more clearly state the standards upon which this discretionary relief may be granted by the Attorney General.

10

The provisions which permit the continuation of up to a 50 per cent mortgage extending far into the future on the quotas of many countries. Under these provisions it is charged that Estonia has its quotas partially mortgaged until the year 2146; 2014 for Greece; Poland, the year 2000, and Turkey, 1964.

It would seem desirable for the Committee on the Judiciary to investigate these complaints and the other critical comments which have developed as a result of the operation of the Immigration and Nationality Law of 1952 with a view to achieving legislation which would be fair and just to all. I shall appreciate it if you will present these comments to the members of the committee and to the chairman of the Senate Committee on the Judiciary.

April 6, 1953

Letter to Vice-President Richard M. Nixon and Speaker of the House Joseph W. Martin, Jr.:

We are all aware of the tragic developments of the past several years which have left countless thousands of individuals homeless refugees in the heart of Europe. In recent months, the number of refugees has been increased by the steady flow of escapees who have braved death to escape from behind the Iron Curtain. These refugees and escapees searching desperately for freedom look to the free world for haven.

In addition, the problem of population pressure continues to be a source of urgent concern in several friendly countries in Europe.

It is imperative that we join with the other nations in helping to find a solution to these grave questions. These refugees, escapees, and distressed peoples now constitute an economic and political threat of constantly growing magnitude. They look to traditional American humanitarian concern for the oppressed. International political considerations are also factors which are involved. We should take reasonable steps to help these people to the extent that we share the obligation of the free world.

Therefore, after consideration of all the points of view which have been presented, I recommend, within the framework of the immigration laws, the enactment of emergency immigration legislation for the special admission of 120,000 immigrants per year for the next two years.

In order to help resolve this current immigration and refugee problem in the tradition of our American policy, I urge that the Congress give this recommendation its earliest consideration.

April 22, 1953

APPENDIX IV

Memorandum on the Visa Problem

PREPARED BY

AMERICAN COMMITTEE FOR CULTURAL FREEDOM (DECEMBER 1952)

The following analysis of the visa problem is concerned primarily with the question of temporary (visitors') visas, and particularly with the troubles that arise for foreign scientists, writers, and intellectuals out of the legislation now incorporated in the Immigration and Nationality Act of 1952, and out of its administration by the State Department. No attempt has been made to discuss the general principles of the law. The purpose of this memorandum is a practical and concrete one: to recommend specific revisions of both the legislation and its method of enforcement, within the framework of the intent of Congress.

This memorandum, prepared by the staff of the American Committee for Cultural Freedom, is based on: discussions with the staff of the Senate Judiciary Committee, members of Congress interested in these matters, members of the State Department, Department of Justice, and Central Intelligence Agency; interviews with foreign diplomatic and intelligence officers, and with foreigners personally involved in visa problems; review of the relevant statutes and regulations; and extended direct participation in a number of visa cases.

THE PROBLEM

Some months ago, the United States Government asked the

Norwegian labor movement to send a delegation of trade union leaders to this country. This delegation was to take the form of a Study Commission, which would examine at firsthand the way of life of the American worker, and which would then report its findings to the Norwegian people. The Norwegian unions nominated nine of their outstanding personalities to the Study Commission. Imagine their consternation when the State Department then informed them that four of their nominees could not be granted visas until their life-histories had been subjected to a more intensive scrutiny!

What was the reason for the State Department's action? One of the nominees, a venerable labor journalist and outstanding anti-Communist, had been affiliated with the Norwegian Communist movement in the early 1920's. A second nominee had visited Russia at the request of the Norwegian labor movement—but had written so hostile a report that the United States Government had reprinted it and distributed it all over the world. The third nominee had been mistaken by the State Department for someone else. The case of the fourth nominee, who had never been connected with any Communist activities, was inexplicable and remains so to this day; presumably he was the victim of a false and malicious "confidential denunciation."

After much delay and unpleasant publicity, all four were cleared for travel in the United States. One can easily imagine, however, that despite the happy ending this incident did not exactly promote good feeling toward America.

Unfortunately, there have been more than a few such incidents, not all of them with happy endings. It is true that, for the kind of bureaucratic civilization in which we live, and in relation to the total number of visitors, they do not cut a large figure. In the past years, tens of thousands of scientists, writers, artists, intellectuals, journalists, students, labor leaders, etc.—far more than in any comparable previous period—have received visas to enter the United States, most of them under governmental grant or subsidy. Nevertheless, it is almost impossible to exaggerate the bad impression created by those cases where an injustice has been suffered. These generally involve prominent members of the intellectual and professional classes, whose status and prestige in their own communities are far higher than that usually accorded to their counterparts in this country. Any senseless affront to them is widely reported in the foreign press and as widely resented by their fellow-citizens. A series of such affronts will cause even the most sympathetic to give credence to the Communist portrait of the United States as a land dominated by a mindless fever of "witch-hunting."

By now, there has been sufficient public turmoil over the visa muddle to elevate what had been a suspicion into a certainty: something is wrong, somewhere. But it is not easy to place one's finger on the exact source of error. Some critics have argued that the State Department has deliberately administered the McCarran Act in such a way as to exaggerate its worst features for the sake of "showing it up." There is, in fact, little evidence to substantiate this accusation. Other critics have asserted that the law itself as it pertains to visitors' visas is governed by an "anti-foreign" xenophobic bias, and that Congress intended surreptitiously to exclude, not only Communists, but also non-Communist liberals, socialists, etc. Here, too, there is no evidence to back up such a charge.

Actually, it would seem that the present situation arises from a complex law which is defective in important respects, and which is administered by a large bureaucratic organization that is not well fitted, either by individual training or institutional precedent, for this novel task.

GENERAL INADEQUACIES OF THE LAW

The Immigration and Nationality Act of 1952, which goes into effect on December 24th, codifies existing legislation in this sphere. With respect to the provisions touching upon visitors' visas, the law has several fairly obvious defects:

(a) Parts are too vaguely worded. For instance, Sec. 212 (a), (27) prohibits the issuing of visas to:

Aliens who seek to enter the United States whether solely,

principally, or incidentally, to engage in activities which would be prejudicial to the public interest, or would endanger the welfare or safety of the United States. This permits of almost any interpretation, and could be used to exclude practically anyone displeasing to a particular administration, party, faction, or even individual official. Similarly, though another section bars aliens who are members of a Communist or other totalitarian "affiliate" or "subsidiary," it is nowhere made clear what is meant by such an "affiliate" or "subsidiary."

(b) The provisions of the law include detailed matters that ought properly to be left in the hands of the administrators. This was done by Congress because of its belief that the Executive and the State Department have been "too soft on Communism." Whatever the meaning or merits of this notion, Congress was mistaken in supposing that it is possible to legislate the detailed administration of so complicated and diverse an operation as the handling of thousands of visa applications in all nations of the world.

(c) The law does not make any clear distinction between visitors' visas and permanent immigration visas.

(d) The law fails to make any special provision for exiles and escapees from nations now under Communist rule.

GENERAL INADEQUACIES OF ADMINISTRATION

With regard to the administration of the law, the following glaring defects immediately strike the eye:

(a) The procedures for getting a visa are unnecessarily slow and cumbersome, braked by too many and too detailed questionnaires, and too mechanical in their failure to allow for atypical cases.

(b) Consuls, like the rest of humanity, are frequently not as good-natured or well-informed as they might be. Consequently, the authority they possess is often wielded irresponsibly.

(c) Because of a fear of Congressional displeasure or investigation, most consular officials will tend to resolve doubts in favor of a "strict" interpretation of the law and of their instructions. The censure they may receive for withholding a visa without good cause is of little weight in comparison with the obloquy they may suffer for granting a visa to someone who, in the opinion of a Congressman, ought not to get it.

(d) Many harrowing difficulties can be traced to the "confidential denunciation," which the ordinary consul rarely can evaluate properly. The very existence of such a confidential denunciation in a dossier—regardless of its validity—is ordinarily enough to cause action to be suspended for a lengthy period. This is the explanation of many cases which have seemed particularly baffling and arbitrary.

(e) Congress has failed to appropriate enough money to the Departments of State and Justice for the rapid handling of visa applications. Much of the infuriating delay that is now experienced is simply the result of the huge backlog of applications which has accumulated.

RECOMMENDED CHANGES IN THE LAW

1) Sec. 212 (a) (27), quoted above, of the Immigration and Nationality Act of 1952, should be eliminated. Its specific content is included in other provisions, and its vague injunctions do not belong in any law.

2) The law should clearly separate the question of temporary (visitors') visas from that of permanent (immigrant) visas. It is both unwise and unnecessary to set up the same stringent requirements for both classes. Temporary visas should be granted with the least possible delay to all applicants, unless there is reason to believe that the applicant intends to make use of his visit to engage in illegal or subversive activities. Membership in the Communist party, or the holding of a leading position in a Communist-front organization, may be interpreted as such a declaration of intention. But even here, there ought to be some room for exceptions, in view of the fact that association with a front organization can mean different things at different places at different times. Especially in countries where the Communists have a mass base, it is not unusual for the names of naive and

prominent businessmen, statesmen, and intellectuals who are definitely non-Communist to turn up on the letterheads of innocuous-appearing, but Communist-sponsored, organizations.

3) There should be special provisions for escapees and exiles from Communist countries. These would take into account the different significance of membership in Communist organizations in Communist, as distinguished from non-Communist countries. While assuring adequate security measures, they should deliberately aim at encouraging escape and at making easier the integration and utilization of escapees.

4) One clause of the new law, while not involving visitors' visas, does affect cultural interchange and is of special concern to such an organization as the American Committee for Cultural Freedom. Until now, a professor at a college or a university, and his immediate family, have been entitled to enter this country for permanent residence as non-quota immigrants. This privilege is abolished by the Immigration and Nationality Act of 1952. Henceforth, professors must wait their turn as ordinary quota immigrants, unless they can prove to the satisfaction of the Attorney General that their services are "needed urgently in the United States." (Sec. 203 (a) (1).) It is impossible to fathom the purpose of this. Certainly, no security problem is at issue, since even as non-quota immigrants these professors would have to meet the standards set up for all immigrants. The only forseeable consequence is that the United States will be depriving itself of distinguished foreign scholars willing to accept permanent posts at American universities. The previous legislation on this matter should be restored.

5) Sec. 212 (a) (28) of the new law represents a big stumbling block. Its main provisions bar aliens who (A) are anarchists, (B) advocate, or are affiliated with an organization that advocates, opposition to all organized government, (C) are members of, or affiliated with, the Communist party or any of its subdivisions and affiliates, (D) advocate the "economic, international, and governmental doctrines of world Communism" or of any other form of totalitarianism, (E) are members of any

organization required to register under the Subversive Activities Control Act of 1950, (F) advocate, or are members of any organization that advocates, "the overthrow by force or violence" of the Government of the United States, (G) write, publish or circulate written or printed matter that calls for the overthrow of the Government of the United States by force, or which teaches "the economic, international, and governmental doctrines of world Communism" or of any other form of totalitarianism, (H) are affiliated with organizations which publish or circulate matter of the kind described in (G). A final section (I) permits the entrance of an alien barred by any of the previous provisions if he can show that he was under sixteen years of age when affiliated with an objectionable organization, or that his membership was involuntary and under constraint, or that since the termination of his membership—and for a period of at least five years—he has been actively opposed to such organizations and their doctrines, or if "the admission of such alien into the United States would be in the public interest."

This section is an outstanding illustration of an attempt by the Immigration and Nationality Act to regulate detailed matters that ought properly to be left in the hands of administrators. It should be drastically amended so that it is more flexible and leaves more to administrative discretion. Mere past, or even present, membership in a single front or semi-front organization —or even in several—ought not in itself to constitute a presumption of subversiveness, though it might be defined as "evidence relevant to a determination of the applicant's admissibility under this paragraph. . ." As has been said above, it is rare that a record of a person's political biography speaks unambiguously for itself; more generally, the significance to be attached to any parts of this record, or to the whole of it, has to be supplied by the informed and intelligent observer—in this case, the consul in charge of issuing visas.

In amending or re-writing this section, the following specific changes should be made:

(a) There should be eliminated from subparagraph (1) the

qualification "when under sixteen years of age" and the definite timing of "for at least five years prior. . . ." The first is superfluous, the second a nuisance by virtue of its being so arbitrary a figure. Moreover, allowance ought to be made for those people, and there are many, who leave the Communist movement and forsake politics altogether. To be sure, it is conceivable that a Communist agent will give the appearance of having become non-political, in order better to deceive. But it is no less conceivable that he will, if necessary, pose as an active anti-Communist. Communist subversion is too protean a force to be calculated and measured definitively by any law, and administrative intelligence will always be needed for the determination of any concrete case.

(b) The clause, which appears twice in subparagraph (1), and which reads: "the admission of such alien into the United States would be in the public interest," should be made to read: "the admission of such alien into the United States would not be counter to the public interest."

(c) The phrase, "economic, international, and governmental doctrines of world Communism or . . . of any other form of totalitarianism," should be avoided on the grounds of vagueness. Its intent would seem to be adequately executed in subparagraph (F), which bars those who "advocate or teach or who are members of or affiliated with any organization" that advocates or teaches the violent overthrow of the Government of the United States. Whether a person is implicated in the Communist, or any other totalitarian, conspiracy is a fact that usually can be objectively determined. To decide whether his beliefs are in accord with Communist or totalitarian doctrine, or what this doctrine precisely is, is infinitely difficult. At the very least, the law should also make a distinction, such as that drawn by the Supreme Court in the case of the Smith Act, between a purely speculative opinion—whether it be Communist, Fascist, Nazi, or Anarchist—held by an individual and a belief that constitutes advocacy of, or incitement to, illegal action.

RECOMMENDED CHANGES IN ADMINISTRATION

1) The main thing is that the quality of consular officials in charge of visas should be improved. All too frequently, these officials are assigned to handle visa applications at the outset of their careers, at a time when they are unversed in the law and in administrative procedure, and when they are generally not very expert in the language, the culture, the history, or the politics of the land in which they work. It is absurd to expect a novice to make sense of the tangled lives of men who have been in, say, the maze of French left-wing politics over a period of decades. What will happen—what has happened—is that he takes refuge in fantastically detailed questionnaires which he is anyway incapable of properly interpreting. (For example: what will such a consul make of an applicant who left the French Communist party in 1936, rejoined it during the war when it was a part of the Resistance, left it again in 1947 in order to join the Rassemblement of General de Gaulle, and whose name has been signed to the Stockholm Peace Appeal? Such veerings and turnings are the rule in France, not the exception.)

Anyone who knows the French—or German or Indian—scene well, and who is politically sophisticated, can determine quite easily whether an applicant is or is not a Communist. (Of course, a secret agent might slip past him—but such an agent can be identified, not by a consul, not by a law, but only by our own counter-intelligence service.) He will at least know whom to ask, and how much store to set by their opinions. At least he will know, as the consul in Liverpool did not, that Arthur Koestler was the author of *The Yogi and the Commissar*, and that the fact of its being dedicated to Michael Polanyi (who was denied a visa) was an item of some political significance. There is simply no substitute, either legal or administrative, for this kind of expert judgment.

There was a happy time when the granting of visas was a tedious and minor clerical assignment, demanding no particular skill. Those days are gone—though not forever, let us hope. As things now stand, the consul in charge of visas has to make very difficult decisions on the basis of very complicated evidence, and his decisions will have a weighty bearing on the success or failure of American foreign policy. Therefore, the need is for first-rate men, and many of them. If the State Department does not now have them, it is inconceivable that it cannot find them.

2) Congress should appropriate sufficient funds, both for the State Department and the Attorney General, to permit adequate staffs for disposing of visa problems more quickly. This might help avoid such farcical episodes as that involving Professor R. E. Peierls of the University of Birmingham, who as a representative of the British government, and holding a diplomatic visa, took part in a top-secret conference in Washington on atomic energy while the consul in Birmingham was waiting for a decision from his superiors on the wisdom of giving Mr. Peierls a visa to attend a scientific convention in Chicago.

3) There is far too much paper work attendant upon the getting of a visa. This is merely the result of the bureaucratic mania for printed forms, and is of no use whatsoever. Why should an applicant have to give the exact address and exact dates of every place of residence since the day he was born? (Question 16, Form LV-2). How many State Department officials or Congressmen can answer such a question honestly and accurately? All such trivial questions should be summarily stricken from application blanks.

4) The improvement of administrative procedures in the field could be aided by the appointment of a temporary roving commission, which would survey the problem and make specific suggestions for its amelioration. This commission should consist of members of the Foreign Service plus business efficiency experts and experts on Communism.

5) A special mechanism should be set up for dealing with visas for attendance at international conferences held within the United States. Perhaps a short-term visa can be issued to cover attendance at accredited conferences and similar meetings. Or, perhaps a special board can be set up within the State Department to deal with proposed lists of foreign delegates to a con-

ference by nonroutine methods. It is apparent, however, that something must be done. It is now almost impossible to plan an international conference in this country, because the sponsors dread the embarrassment of inviting a distinguished guest and of having his request for a visa turned down.

CONCLUSION

One of the favorite bits of propaganda of an anti-Communist group in France has been to post ironic placards, urging French Communists to visit "the Soviet Paradise," and instructing them to apply for a visa at the Soviet Embassy in Paris. This witty comment on the existence of the Iron Curtain was well appreciated by the average Frenchman. Recently, an anti-Communist journalist in Paris, who had been denied an American visa because he belonged to the Communist Youth movement more than two decades ago, received one of these placards in the mail, with the word "Soviet" crossed out and the word "American" written above it.

What could he say? And what can we, as Americans, say to him?

We know that the visa problem was not created by arbitrary malice on the part of Congressmen or State Department officials. It is but one reflection, and not by far the largest, of the stresses and strains which this free country is suffering as a result of its determination to resist Communist totalitarianism.

Nevertheless, it is a problem whose power of irritation is out of all proportion to its dimensions. Throughout the world, in universities, laboratories, libraries, and editorial offices, we have friends and potential friends whom we have, in effect, insulted and shamed. The worst of it all is that it needn't have happened —that no one really wanted the visa muddle we now flounder in. It was the unintended consequence of over-zealous legislation compounded by over-cautious administration.

This memorandum has made specific suggestions which, we believe, will eliminate the majority of nasty situations that now arise so frequently. We urge Congress and the State Department to act upon them with all possible haste.

APPENDIX V

Table of Immigrant Quotas under 1952 Law

On June 30, 1952, President Truman proclaimed the following immigration quotas under the new law (McCarran-Walter Act):[1]

Britain and Northern Ireland	65,361	Denmark	1,175
Germany	25,814	Yugoslavia	933
Ireland (Eire)	17,756	Hungary	865
Poland	6,488	Finland	566
Italy	5,645	Portugal	438
Sweden	3,295	Lithuania	384
Netherlands	3,136	Greece	308
France	3,069	Rumania	289
Czechoslovakia	2,859	Spain	250
Russia	2,679	Latvia	235
Norway	2,364	Turkey	225
Switzerland	1,698	Japan	185
Austria	1,405	Estonia	115
Belgium	1,297	China (racial)	105

Quotas of 100 persons annually:

Afghanistan, Albania, Andorra, Arabian Peninsula, Australia, Bhutan, Bulgaria, Burma, Cambodia, Cameroons (British),

[1] *New York Times,* July 1, 1952. See also *Whom We Shall Welcome,* Report of President's Commission on Immigration and Naturalization (1953), 99-101.

Cameroun (French), Ceylon, China, Danzig, Egypt, Ethiopia, Iceland, India, Indonesia, Iran, Iraq, Israel, Jordan, Korea, Laos, Lebanon, Liberia, Libya, Liechtenstein, Luxembourg, Monaco, Morocco, Muscat (Oman), Nauru (Australian), Nepal, New Guinea (Australian), New Zealand, Pacific Islands (U.S.), Pakistan, Palestine (Arab), Philippines, Ruanda-Urundi (Belgian), San Marino, Saudi Arabia, Somaliland (Italian), Southwest Africa, Syria, Tanganyika (British), Thailand, Togo (French), Togoland (British), Trieste, Union of South Africa, Vietnam, Western Samoa (New Zealand), Yemen.

APPENDIX VI

ALIENS DEPORTED AND ALIENS DEPARTING VOLUNTARILY UNDER PROCEEDINGS: YEARS ENDED JUNE 30, 1892 TO 1950

Period	Total	Aliens deported	Aliens departing voluntarily [1] under proceedings
1892 – 1950	1,999,177	362,689	1,636,488
1892 – 1900	3,127	3,127	—
1901 – 1910	11,558	11,558	—
1911 – 1920	27,912	27,912	—
1921 – 1930	164,390	92,157	72,233
1921....	4,517	4,517	—
1922....	4,345	4,345	—
1923....	3,661	3,661	—
1924....	6,409	6,409	—
1925....	9,495	9,495	—
1926....	10,904	10,904	—
1927....	26,674	11,662	15,012
1928....	31,571	11,625	19,946
1929....	38,796	12,908	25,888
1930....	28,018	16,631	11,387
1931 – 1940	210,416	117,086	93,330
1931....	29,861	18,142	11,719
1932....	30,201	19,426	10,775
1933....	30,212	19,865	10,347
1934....	16,889	8,879	8,010
1935....	16,297	8,319	7,978
1936....	17,446	9,195	8,251
1937....	17,617	8,829	8,788
1938....	18,553	9,275	9,278
1939....	17,792	8,202	9,590
1940....	15,548	6,954	8,594
1941 – 1950	1,581,774	110,849	1,470,925
1941....	10,938	4,407	6,531
1942....	10,613	3,709	6,904
1943....	16,154	4,207	11,947
1944....	39,449	7,179	32,270
1945....	80,760	11,270	69,490
1946....	116,320	14,375	101,945
1947....	214,543	18,663	195,880
1948....	217,555	20,371	197,184
1949....	296,337	20,040	276,297
1950....	579,105	6,628	572,477

[1] Voluntary departures of aliens under proceedings first recorded in 1927.
Source: United States Department of Justice, Immigration and Naturalization Service.

APPENDIX VII

Certificates of Naturalization Cancelled

1907-1951

Judgments of Naturalization Revoked, Fiscal years 1907-1951

1907-1946	18,718	1947	94
1907-1910	1,861	1948	163
1911-1920	2,043	1949	184
1921-1930	4,127	1950	415
1931-1940	8,025	1951	403
1941-1946	2,662		

Source: United States Department of Justice, Immigration and Naturalization Service.

Index

INDEX

INDEX

INDEX

INDEX

INDEX

www.ingramcontent.com/pod-product-compliance
Ingram Content Group UK Ltd.
Pitfield, Milton Keynes, MK11 3LW, UK
UKHW021030041026
15470UKWH00013B/1086

9 780837 195568